Thunderbolt

The Republic P-47 Thunderbolt in the European Theater

By Ernest R. McDowell
Color by Don Greer

squadron/signal publications

(Cover) P-47s of the 82nd Fighter Squadron, 78th Fighter Group locate and attack a German column moving up to engage Allied ground forces in Normandy during June of 1944. Such operations severely hampered the German's ability to adequately resupply the battlefield.

Acknowledgements

Al Anderson	Art Krieger
Ray Bain	R. E. Kuhnert
Theo Bennett	John Lambert
Peter M. Bowers	Jim Lansdale
Col J. Ward Boyce	Don Madden
Gil C. Burns	A. F. Maltbie
James V. Crow	Chuck Mann
Carlos E. Dannacher	N. A. Nilsson
Larry Davis	James Quernes
Fred C. Dickey, Jr.	Paul Quilty
Jeffrey L. Ethell	P. W. Robinson
R. Fairbanks	Kenn C. Rust
Santiago Flores	Col C. L. Sluder
Garry L. Fry	Sam L. Sox
James F. Gallagher	John Stanaway
D. F. Gelhaus	Pat Stein
Steve Gotes	L. D. Volkmer
W. A. Grabowski	David Weatherill
Norris Graser	Stan Wilson
Marc Hamel	Col Stanley J. Wyglendowski
R. M. Harding	USAAF
William N. Hess	USAF Museum
A. A. Hitch	355th Fighter Group
Arthur Houston	Association
W. J. Jahnke	
Robert C. Jones	
Ted Koston	

ISBN 0-89747-393-0

If you have any photographs of aircraft, armor, soldiers or ships of any nation, particularly wartime snapshots, why not share them with us and help make Squadron/Signal's books all the more interesting and complete in the future. Any photograph sent to us will be copied and the original returned. The donor will be fully credited for any photos used. Please send them to:

Squadron/Signal Publications, Inc.
1115 Crowley Drive.
Carrollton, TX 75011-501010

Если у вас есть фотографии самолетов, вооружения, солдат или кораблей любой страны, особенно, снимки времен войны, поделитесь с нами и помогите сделать новые книги издательства Эскадрон/Сигнал еще интереснее. Мы переснимем ваши фотографии и вернем оригиналы. Имена приславших снимки будут сопровождать все опубликованные фотографии. Пожалуйста, присылайте фотографии по адресу:

Squadron/Signal Publications, Inc.
1115 Crowley Drive.
Carrollton, TX 75011-501010

軍用機、装甲車両、兵士、軍艦などの写真を所持しておられる方は いらっしゃいませんか？どの国の ものでも結構です。作戦中に撮影されたものが特に良いのです。Squadron/Signal社の出版する刊行物 において、このような写真は内容を一層充実し、興味深くすることができます。当方にお送り頂いた 写真は、複写の後お返しいたします。出版物中に写真を使用した場合は、必ず提供者のお名前を明記 させて頂きます。お写真は下記にご送付ください。

Squadron/Signal Publications, Inc.
1115 Crowley Drive.
Carrollton, TX 75011-501010

(Previous Page) Republic Aviation Company test pilots fly brand new P-47D-25-REs over Long Island NY during 1944. Most of these aircraft retained their natural metal schemes when they reached the front. (Republic)

Introduction

The Republic P-47 Thunderbolt was designed by Alexander Kartvelli, a former World War I Russian artillery officer. Kartvelli was a driving force behind the resurgent Republic Aviation — formerly Seversky Aircraft. Alexander Kartvelli ignored the trends of the 1930s towards liquid-cooled engines and created the heavyweight radial-engined champion of WW II fighters. The P-47 was designed as a high altitude interceptor and made its first flight on 6 May 1941. It was the largest and heaviest single-engined fighter built up to that time. It was powered by a 2000 hp turbo-supercharged Pratt & Whitney Double Wasp engine turning a four-bladed variable pitch propeller. A paddle-bladed propeller added later turned the aircraft into an all altitude fighter. During its flight tests it achieved a speed of 412 miles per hour at 25,000 feet.

The P-47 was flown by many of the US Army Air Force's top aces — among them Col Francis Gabreski with 31 victories, Capt Robert S. Johnson with 27, Col Neel Kearby with 22, Capt Fred Christensen, 21.5, and Col Hubert Zemke with 20. Their efforts alone ensured the Thunderbolt's place in history as a fighter. Two P-47 pilots were awarded the Medal of Honor while flying the Thunderbolt. Col Neel Kearby destroyed six Japanese aircraft on a single mission and Lt Raymond L. Knight received a posthumous Medal of Honor for destroying 20 German aircraft on the ground over a two day period. Lt Knight lost his life when his P-47 was hit by flak on his last pass over an enemy airfield and he was unable to clear a mountain while returning to base.

The P-47 was affectionately known as the 'Jug' — short for Juggernaut — and there have been a number of anecdotes as to how the P-47 picked up the nickname. The name Juggernaut is derived from an ancient Sanskrit word. During a Hindu religious celebration a large stone idol of the god Jagannatha was placed on rollers and the faithful would throw themselves beneath the rollers to be crushed. The word 'Juggernaut' signifies a terrible, irresistible force — an apt description of the P-47.

P-47 Thunderbolts in Europe flew 423,435 sorties — almost twice as many as any other US fighter. The weight of bombs dropped — 113,939 tons —was almost triple that of all other fighters combined. The 3077 P-47s lost in combat accounted for almost one third of all US fighters lost in action. In turn, P-47 pilots shot down 3082 enemy aircraft in the air and destroyed a further 3203 on the ground. Their combat mission loss rate was a meager 0.7% per sortie. In the Pacific Theater P-47 pilots shot down an additional 713 enemy aircraft to rank third among US Army fighters, but only sixth if Navy fighters are included. P-47s flying in all theaters dropped 132,000 tons of bombs, expended 135 million rounds of fifty caliber ammunition, and fired 60,000 rockets throughout the war.

The P-47 had a wingspan of 40 feet, 9 and 3/4 inches, while the P-47N, the last variant to see operational service, had a span of 42 feet 7 inches. Lengths varied from 35 feet, 3 and 1/4 inches to 36 feet, 4 inches. The P-47's maximum weight ranged from 13,360 pounds to 20,700 pounds, while its maximum speed went from 429 mph at 27,000 feet to 460 mph at 30,000 feet. The P-47's service ceiling was between 42,000 feet and 43,000 feet. The seven-ton plus P-47 consumed gasoline at the rate of 90-130 gallons per hour at cruising speed.

The P-47 began its war in Europe escorting bombers taking the war to the Axis heartland. During the last half of the war, the P-47 transitioned into the role of low-level tactical support, a role in which it had no peer. Indeed, the last sight and sound of many Axis soldiers and airmen was the flash and roar of the Republic P-47 Thunderbolt.

P-47Bs (later RP-47B - for Restricted) of the 56th Fighter Group cruise over the New York coastline. The 'B' model was used only for training and testing and did not see combat. These fighters are camouflaged in olive drab upper surfaces and neutral gray under surfaces with medium green splotching along the leading and trailing edges of the wings and tail. (Republic)

The 8th Air Force

The US 8th Air Force began as the VIII Bomber Command on 19 January 1942 and was activated in the United States on 1 February 1942. An advanced detachment was sent to England on 23 February while other units followed during the spring. Their mission was to use the strategic bombardment of military and industrial complexes as a means of carrying the war into the Axis heartland. The VIII Bomber Command was redesignated the 8th Air Force on 22 February 1944 *(for continuity 8th AF will be used throughout this book - ed.)*. Strategic bombing operations continued until the end of the war in Europe on 8 May 1945. The 8th AF was transferred (on paper) to Okinawa on 16 July 1945 for the coming invasion of Japan although no actual movement of men or materiel had taken place before the war ended in August.

The 8th AF was primarily a strategic bomber force, however it was understood that the bombers would need to be escorted to and from the target. Consequently, the 8th was assigned numerous fighter groups flying Lockheed P-38 Lightnings and Republic's P-47 Thunderbolt. Both fighters played an extensive role in escorting the bombers, conducting fighter sweeps, and flying decoy missions — all with the aim of keeping Luftwaffe fighters away from the bombers. During mid-1943, the Jug also flew its first ground attack missions against Luftwaffe airfields and flak batteries.

Eleven P-47 groups were assigned to the 8th Air Force during the war. Only one group, the 56th Fighter Group, flew Thunderbolts throughout the war. All of the other groups eventually converted to the North American P-51 Mustang when they became available since it was more suited for escorting long-range bombers. However, it would be difficult to argue that the P-47 did not more than hold its own against the Luftwaffe when one considers the record of the 56th Fighter Group — 'Zemke's Wolf Pack' — whose 674.5 air-to-air victories ranked first in the 8th. The 56th FG scored a further 311 kills on the ground (ranking them fourth) and lost only 129 P-47s in combat.

During the period from August of 1942 through May of 1945 Thunderbolts of the 8th Air Force claimed a total of 1563 enemy aircraft destroyed in the air. During the same period, 529 P-47s were lost in combat, 44 were listed as missing, another 176 suffered Category B damage, 25 became war weary, and 74 had to be salvaged due to non-operational causes. Some 69 Thunderbolt pilots had to bail out or ditch over water with 27 being rescued — a 60% loss rate in that category. Although the 8th Air Force counted ground kills, only air-to-air victories are counted here since no reliable ground kill records could be located. A few of the air-to-air kills may be questionable since, in most cases, no firm date for the last P-47 mission could be found after a group switched to the P-51. Furthermore, some groups flew both fighters in combat as they transitioned from the P-47 to the P-51. Some units sent up one P-51 squadron and two P-47 squadrons on the same mission, while others alternated the two during the first few missions of the transition. One group continued to put up a flight of four Thunderbolts well after the majority of the group was flying Mustangs.

It is interesting that the seven top aces of the 56th FG had a combined victory total of 149, a record not matched by any other group regardless of what aircraft they flew. Additionally, 19 of the top 25 aces flew the P-47 during their combat careers and the two top scoring American aces — Gabreski and Johnson — flew only the Thunderbolt.

4th Fighter Group

The 4th Fighter Group was authorized on 22 August 1942 and activated in England on 12 September. The nucleus of the group consisted of ex-members of the RAF Eagle Squadrons — US citizens flying for the British Royal Air Force. The three Eagle Squadrons (Nos 71, 121, and 133) became the 334th, 335th, and 336th Fighter Squadrons of the 4th FG. In the beginning the 4th FG flew Spitfires, but began the transition to the P-47 during January of 1943. The switch was unpopular with the pilots at first.

The transition from the lightweight Spitfire to Republic's heavyweight 'Jug' was completed during March of 1943. The first full P-47 mission was flown on 15 April 1943. Maj Don Blakeslee downed a Focke-Wulf Fw 190 near Knocke-Ostend, Belgium for the first victory scored by a P-47. On the same mission Capt Lee Gover, Lt Col Chesley G. Peterson, and Lt Robert A. Boocke also bagged Fw 190s. Thereafter the Group flew Ramrod (Escort), Rodeo (Decoy), Rhubarb (low level strafing) and Roadstead (anti-shipping and ports) missions. They received a Distinguished Unit Citation (DUC) for destroying enemy aircraft during March and April of 1943 in France.

The last Thunderbolt mission by the 4th FG was flown on 25 February 1944 (a period known as Big Week) during a deep penetration mission to Sedan-Stuttgart, Germany. Five Fw 190s were destroyed without loss. The 4th FG then converted to the North American P-51 Mustang.

The 4th FG was credited with 125 victories against only 17 losses while flying the Thunderbolt. The 334th FS led the scoring with 52.5, the 335th FS followed with 39, and the 336th claimed 29.5. The Headquarters Flight added four more. Lt Duane W. Beeson of the 334th FS was the Group's top ace with 10 kills. Capts Roy Evans and James J.

Capt Williard W. Millikan flew *Missouri Mauler*, a P-47C-2-RA (41-6180). Millikan was a 15 victory ace with the 336th FS, 4th FG. The aircraft carries the white cowl ring and tail bands used to identify the P-47 in the air. (Garry L. Fry)

WD*K, a P-47C-5-RE of the 335th FS, 4th FG, collided with another P-47 during takeoff on 15 January 1944 — losing most of its right wing and damaging its tail. (Garry L. Fry)

Clark also became aces with the Jug, but each had had a previous victory while flying Spitfires. Capt Henry Miller got his five with the P-47 and Maj James A. Goodson led the 336th squadron with his five victories. Several of the Group's aces scored kills in the P-47 Thunderbolt.

The 4th FG's P-47Cs and Ds were painted in the standard factory scheme of olive drab upper surfaces with neutral gray under surfaces. On 20 February 1943 the unit was ordered to paint a white band on the cowling to avoid it being mistaken for the Luftwaffe's Fw 190. The white cowl ring was augmented by white bands painted on both vertical and horizontal tail surfaces. The **334th FS** used **QP** as its code, the **335th** was assigned **WD**, and the **336th** was given **VF**. The squadron codes were painted in white on both fuselage sides. No special group or squadron markings were used. The serial numbers on the vertical tail surfaces were usually painted yellow.

56th Fighter Group

The 56th FG began as the 56th Pursuit Group (Interceptor) on 20 November 1940 and was activated on 15 January 1941. The Group trained on the Bell P-39 and Curtiss P-40, but switched to the Republic P-47 after it was redesignated the 56th Fighter Group in May of 1942. Combat training lasted throughout the summer and fall of 1943. The Group and its three fighter squadrons — the 61st, 62nd, and 63rd — moved to Kings Cliffe, England and the VIII Bomber Command during December of 1942 and January of 1943. The Group would occupy three other bases during its stay in England.

The Group's first mission — a fighter sweep to the St Omer, France area — was flown on 13 April 1943. Apart from the Group Commander, Col Hubert Zemke, having to abort due to an oxygen system failure, the mission was uneventful. The 56th FG settled into the role of flying escort missions, fighter sweeps, and the occasional attack on Luftwaffe airfields. The Group's first victory occurred on 12 June 1943 when Capt Walter Cook claimed an Fw 190 over Ypres, France. On 17 August Majors G. W. Johnson and G. Schultz scored the first triple kills and on 19 August 1943 Maj Johnson became the first ace of the 56th FG. 1Lts Walker 'Bud' Mahurin of the 63rd FS and E. McCauley both received Silver Stars on 1 October, while Col Zempke made ace the next day and received a British DFC. On 8 October Lt Mahurin became the top scoring ace in the ETO with 20 victories. On 17 October Maj Schultz received the Group's first Distinguished Service Cross (DSC). October became known as 'medal month'. On 25 November 1943 the group flew over 15 fighter-bomber missions to the St. Omer region — an indication of the P-47's future role in the war against Germany.

The 56th FG scored its 200th victory on 30 January 1944. The first 150 gallon belly drop tanks were received on 20 February which allowed the Group to range farther into Germany while escorting the bombers. From 20 February to 9 March, the Group was so engaged that its efforts resulted in the Group's first Distinguished Unit Citation (DUC). By March of 1944, the Thunderbolt's engines were equipped with water injection — an improvement that provided short term bursts of additional power for use in dogfights. Capt Robert S. Johnson took over the lead in kills when he destroyed three German fighters on 15 March 1944 and raised his total score to 21.

On 19 May 1944 the 56th began to receive the new P-47D-25 equipped with a bubble canopy. These new aircraft flew side-by-side with the older P-47 'Razorbacks'. On 30 May Col Zempke, flying in a Lockheed P-38 Droopsnoot, led the Group's Jugs on a mission to the Creil Bridge in France with each accompanying Thunderbolt carrying a single 1,000 lb bomb. However, the flak barrage at the Creil Bridge was so intense the 56th was forced to switch targets. The fighters targeted the Chantilly Bridge and dropped three of its spans.

On 6 June 1944 the 56th FG was engaged in supporting OPERATION OVERLORD — the Allied invasion of Normandy, France. Eight missions were flown that day, all of them close support. During the month of June the Group continued to support the invasion forces and lost nine pilots in combat. Three of these pilots managed to bail out and return to the Group.

On 5 July 1944 Col Francis Gabreski became the top ace in the ETO when he scored his 28th kill and passed Robert S. Johnson's total of 27. On 12 August Col Zemke was transferred to the 479th FG to oversee that Group's transition from P-38s to P-51s. He was replaced by Col David Schilling, a long time member of the Group. Under Schilling the Group received its second DUC for anti-aircraft suppression strikes when they knocked out 20 gun positions in Holland on 17 September. On 1 November Lt Walter R. Groce of the 63rd FS was given a half kill when he and six other pilots cornered and destroyed a Luftwaffe Me 262 jet fighter that had just flamed a P-51. Col Schilling passed Col Gabreski as the ETO's top ace on 23 December 1944 with 34.5 victories (including ground kills).

Operations and qualitative improvements continued into the new year. On 17 February 1945 the 63rd FS replaced their P-47Ds with the newer, more powerful, and longer ranging P-47Ms. One month later, on 21 April 1945, the Group flew its last combat mission.

During its operational career the 56th FG produced 49 aces and, in

Miss Plainfield **was a P-47D-1-RE flown by Lt Spiros N. (Steve) Pisanos of the 334th FS, 4th FG. The aircraft carries the early style US insignia in six positions and the aircraft code letter 'D' is repeated in black under the cowl ring. (D.W. Weatherill)**

Flt Lt Witold Lanowski, an ex-RAF Eagle Squadron pilot assigned to the 56th Fighter Group's 61st FS, flew an overall matte black P-47M-1-RE (44-21108) with a red cowl band, canopy frame, and code letters. Lanowski's personal insignia was a fist crushing an Me 109 superimposed on the Polish Air Force insignia. (R.C. Jones)

Lt Col Joseph Myers' P-47D-27-RA rests on the Bassingbourn flight-line. Myers was assigned to the 82nd FS, 78th FG and received a half kill for assisting in the destruction of an Me 262. (USAAF)

Francis Gabreski and Bob Johnson, had the two top aces in the ETO with 28 and 27 aerial victories respectively. The 56th compiled an amazing statistical record flying 447 combat missions totaling 19,391 sorties and 64,302 combat hours. They expended over 3 million rounds of ammunition, 59 rockets, and dropped 1,356,000 pounds of bombs. The statistics were earned the hard way. The group suffered 150 casualties with nine killed in action and 29 wounded. One hundred and twenty-nine pilots were listed as missing in action and 35 were prisoners of war. Eight pilots downed in combat evaded capture and returned to duty. The 56th FG racked up a score of 677.5 aerial victories, 58 probables, and 324 ground kills. The 62nd FS led the Group with 224 kills, followed by the 61st with 219, the 63rd with 167.5, and the Headquarters Flight with an additional 67.

The Group's aircraft were initially camouflaged in olive drab and neutral gray with a white cowl ring, although the cowl ring was painted red after 15 February 1944. The olive drab and neutral gray schemes gradually gave way to natural metal during the course of 1944. Later, the **61st FS** added red rudders and painted their **HV** code letters in red with white outlines. The **62nd** used the code letters **LM**. Their letters and rudders were painted yellow. The **63rd FS** painted its rudders blue, but their **UN** code letters were left in natural metal. As the Group's reputation grew, the Squadrons began to adopt individual, and non-standard, squadron camouflage schemes. The 61st FS selected midnight blue upper surfaces, the 62nd FS picked medium sea gray and dark green, and the 63rd adopted a dark French blue and a light azure blue. The under surfaces were usually left in natural metal.

(Above) HL*C was a 'War Weary' P-47D-15-RE (denoted by the 'WW' above the serial number) assigned to the 83rd FS, 78th FG. The cowling was encircled with black and white checks, the cowl flaps were painted red, and the rudder was painted white with a red outline. (Larry Davis)

(Below) SSgts Thurman Schreel and Charles Taylor of the 56th FG received permission to modify a 'War Weary' P-47D-11-RE into a two-seat general service aircraft. Aside from the usual liaison and fast transport work, CATEGORY "E" was used operationally for four radar missions during April of 1945. Schreel and Taylor received a Bronze Star for their efforts.

78th Fighter Group

The formation of the 78th Pursuit Group was authorized on 13 January 1942 with the Group being activated on 9 February at Baer Field, Indiana. The Group moved to California during April and May of 1942 and immediately began training on Lockheed P-38 Lightnings. Under the command of Maj Arman Peterson, the 78th FG arrived at Goxhall, England on 1 December 1942. The unit had hardly begun to work up to combat readiness when it lost its aircraft and a number of pilots to the ongoing North African campaign.

The first P-47s began to arrive on 28 January 1943. After completing familiarization training the 78th moved to Duxford on 3 April 1943. It flew its first mission ten days later when the Group's 82nd and 83rd Fighter Squadrons joined the 4th Fighter Group in a fighter sweep over the French coast near St Omer. This mission was uneventful until Lt Col Joe Dickman's Jug suffered engine failure and he had to bail out over the channel. Lt Col Dickman was picked up by an Air-Sea Rescue boat.

On 28 May 1943 Capt Alvin "Max" Jucheim was involved in a mid-air collision with a P-51 of the 363rd Fighter Group while flying at 22,000 feet over Gardelegen, Germany. The impact sheared off part of the P-47's wing and threw the heavy fighter into a spin. The Mustang went straight in and exploded. Jucheim managed to bail out only to become a helpless human target as an Me 109 dived on his chute. Luckily two of Jucheim's squadron mates stayed around to cover his descent and they quickly closed in on the German fighter and shot it down — William McDermott getting credit for the kill. Jucheim became a POW after earning the distinction of being strafed while in his parachute.

On 30 July 1943 the Group claimed 16 enemy aircraft with Capt Charles P. London destroying an Me 109 and Fw 190 to become the first 8th Air Force ace. Maj Eugene P. Roberts was credited with the 78th's first triple kill. On the return flight 1Lt Quince L. Brown came across a train while flying at low level and shot it up. He is generally credited with the 8th AF's first P-47 strafing attack. Another famous

first for the 78th FG came on 28 August 1944 when 2Lt Manford O. Croy, Jr. and Major Joseph Myers shared credit for shooting down the first Me 262 jet fighter claimed by the 8th Air Force. The Me 262, flown by Oberfeldwebel H. Layer, was assigned to Kommando Schenk. Layer managed to get out of the aircraft, but was apparently wounded by Cory as he fled on foot.

The 78th FG spent the summer of 1944 supporting the Normandy landings and the subsequent Allied breakout at St Lo. The Group was awarded a DUC for their further support during the Allied airborne attack (OPERATION MARKET GARDEN) on Holland during September of 1944. The 78th FG converted to P-51 Mustangs during December of 1944.

While flying the P-47 the Group completed 16,621 sorties, shot down 239.5 enemy aircraft, probably destroyed another 22, and damaged 119 in the air. The Group claimed another 142 destroyed, 117 damaged, and 2 probables on the ground. Overall the 78th FG suffered 167 MIAs during the 450 missions flown. The 78th FG added a further 99 aerial kills while flying the Mustang. The Group had 10 P-47 aces (counting only aerial kills). The 84th FS led with 29 victories divided among aces Maj Q. L. Brown (12.5), Capt J. W. Wilkson (6), Capt P. B. Pompetti (5.5) and Maj J. C. Price (5). The HQ Flight had 15 divided among aces Lt Col B. P. Roberts with nine and Lt Col J. J. Oberhansly with six. The 83rd FS followed with 14 by aces Capt A. M. Jucheim (9) and Capt C. P. London (5). The 82nd FS's, Capt J. Hockery (7) and 1Lt G. M. Turley (6) rounded out the Group's roster of aces.

The 78th FG's P-47s were painted in the standard olive drab over neutral gray camouflage scheme worn by most of the 8th AF's fighter groups until natural metal finishes became predominant. Group markings consisted of the code letter **MX** for the **82nd squadron**, **HL** for the **83rd**, and **WZ** for the **84th**. Originally the cowl rings were painted white as a theater marking. Black and white checkerboard cowls were added during April of 1944. During November of 1944, the rudders were painted in squadron colors — red for the 82nd, white for the 83rd, and black for the 84th. Personal markings, when applied, were usually painted on the fuselage in the vicinity of the cockpit.

An oil-soaked HL*J — a P-47D-22-RE of the 83rd FS, 78th FG — sits in the grass awaiting the attention of the ground crew. Natural metal P-47s used black recognition bands on the tail versus the white bands found on camouflaged P-47s. (USAAF)

(Above) Maj Jack C. Price commanded the 84th FS, 78th FG while flying *Feather Merchant II*, a P47D-6-RE (42-74641). Five kill markings are painted under the canopy sill. (Author's Collection)

(Below) Capt Richard A. Hewitt of the 82nd FS, 78th FG flew P-47D-25-RE (MX*E) on his second tour of duty. The fighter has full invasion stripes and oversized national insignia under both wings. (Author's Collection)

352nd Fighter Group

The 352nd Fighter Group was authorized on 29 September 1942 and activated at Mitchell Field, New York on 1 October 1942. It was moved to Bradley Field, Connecticut that same day where it became a part of the Air Defense Command. On 9 March 1943 the Group moved to Republic Field at Farmingdale, NY where it conducted additional training on the P-47. On 1 July the Group embarked on the liner *Queen Elizabeth* and arrived in England on 6 July. The Group and it's three fighter squadrons (328th FS, 486th FS, and 487th FS) settled in at Bodney on 8 July under the command of Col Joseph L. Mason. Mason would command the Group until it converted to the P-51.

The 352nd FG flew its first P-47 mission on 9 September 1943 and immediately settled into its primary role as a bomber escort. Maj John C. Meyer of the 487th FS drew first blood for the Group on 26 November 1943 when he shot down an Me 109. It was the first of his four victories scored while flying the Jug. On 29 January 1944 Capt George B. Preddy scored his third victory when he destroyed an Me 109. On the return flight Preddy took a flak hit in the engine while over Belgium and had to bail out over the English Channel. He was rescued by an RAF Supermarine Walrus seaplane which was damaged while landing on the choppy seas. An ASR launch was called and arrived to take the Walrus under tow. The Walrus pilot was from Darwin, Australia and, during the course of conversation, he learned that Preddy had been stationed near Darwin with the 49th Fighter Group and that they shared a number of mutual friends in Darwin.

The 352nd FG, like many groups in the 8th AF, took part in 'Big Week' — a series of heavy bombing attacks on the Luftwaffe's fighter production facilities during 20 to 25 February 1944. Two months later, in April of 1944, the Group flew its final P-47 mission.

The 352nd FG accumulated 86 victories while flying the P-47. The 328th FS led with 36, the 487th FS was close behind with 33, the 486th followed with 15, and the HQ Flight trailed with a respectable score of 11 kills. The 352nd FS produced three Jug aces: Capt Virgil C. Meroney of the 487th with seven and Maj John C. Meyer (also from the 487th) and Col Joe L. Mason, the Group Commander, with five each.

The Group's P-47Ds were painted in olive drab over neutral gray. The **328th FS** was assigned the letter code **PE**, the **486th** used **PZ**, and the **487th** wore **HO**. No special group markings were used beyond the standard white cowl rings and tail bands used to identify the aircraft as P-47s rather than Fw 190s.

Lt Col Joel Mason's P-47D-5-RE (PZ*M) was named *"GENA THIS IS IT"* after his wife. Mason was the Commanding Officer of the 486th FS, 352nd FG. A five hundred pound bomb is mounted on the fuselage centerline. (Sam Sox)

HO*W was a P-47D-2-RE damaged by an exploding bomb and covered with debris. The fighter, assigned to the 487th FS, 352nd FG, was later repaired.

Lt J. C. Coleman flew *Mavoureen*, a P-47D-3-RA, during the late summer of 1943. *Mavoureen* wears a red surround around the fuselage insignia and is equipped with a 75 gallon P-40 style drop tank. Coleman was assigned to the 328th FS, 352nd FG.

(Above) 1Lt Donald Y. Whinnem of the 486th FS, 352nd FG scored a lone victory on 21 April 1944. Whinnem didn't get credit for shooting down Maj Glenn T. Eagleston, the 9th AF's leading ace. Eagleston was working over Whinnem's Flight Leader, Lt Alfred L. Marshall, while mistaking Marshall's Jug for an Fw 190. Whinnem shot up Eagleston's P-51 Mustang to the point where Eagleston was forced to bail out.

(Below) Another day in England. Ground crews prepare PZ*K, a razorback P-47D, for another mission on a typical foggy day at Bodney. The fighter was assigned to the 486th FS, 352nd FG and wears the standard olive drab and neutral gray camouflage scheme with a white cowl ring and tail identification bands. The code letters were also painted white.

353rd Fighter Group

The 353rd Fighter Group was authorized on 29 September 1942 and activated on 1 October at Mitchell Field, New York. Three squadrons (the 350th, 351st, and 352nd) were assigned to the Group and all were based at Richmond Army Air Base, Virginia to begin training on P-40s. The Group converted to P-47s while serving in the Air Defense Sector. The Group moved to Goxhill, England and the 8th AF during the late spring of 1943. Lt Col Joseph A. Morris commanded the Group until he was reported missing in action on 16 August 1943 — a mere four days after the Group began combat operations.

From August of 1943 until February of 1944 the Group was engaged in bomber escort missions. During 20 to 25 February they took part in 'Big Week' and flew missions against the Luftwaffe and its supporting industries. The 353rd FG pioneered P-47 dive bombing and close support techniques later adopted by both the 8th and 9th Air Forces. During the Normandy invasion the Group flew cover over the beachhead. The Group provided close air support when the Allied troops moved inland after the breakout at St. Lo in July of 1944. During the Airborne invasion of Holland the Group received a DUC for protecting the bombers and transports by strafing and bombing ground targets from 17 through 23 September. The 353rd Fighter Group transitioned to P-51 Mustangs during October of 1944.

The 353rd Fighter Group destroyed 181.5 enemy aircraft while flying the P-47. The 350th FS claimed 62.5, the 351st was credited with 61, and the 352nd scored 58. Lt Col Kenneth W. Gallup led the 350th FS with nine kills, while Lt William F. Tanner had five. The 351st FS was led by Maj Walter C. Beckham. Beckham shot down 18 enemy aircraft while flying his P-47 *Little Demon*. When Beckham was shot down he was the leading ace of the 8th AF. Capt Orville A. Maguire scored five of his seven kills in the Jug and was second to Beckham in the 351st. The 352nd FS had three pilots, 1Lt William Streit, 1Lt Robert A. Newman, and 1Lt Jesse W. Gonnam, who just missed becoming aces with 4.5 victories each.

The early Group P-47s were camouflaged in olive drab and neutral gray. The later P-47D-21s arrived in a natural metal finish. Some of

Prudence was a late production P-47D (LH*S) flown by Maj William F. Tanner of the 350th FS, 353rd FG. Tanner scored 5.5 victories during the war.

these were camouflaged in dark green or a dark green and gray disruptive scheme. Squadron code letters were **LH** for the **350th**, **YJ** for the **351st**, and **SX** for the **352nd**. The Group marking consisted of square or diamond shaped black and yellow checkers on the cowls.

P-47D-2-RE (SX*R) was one of the first P-47s assigned to the 352nd FG during the spring of 1943. The fuselage insignia has the white bars added during the spring of 1943, but lacks the red surround introduced during the summer of 1943. The red surround would later be deleted during the early fall of 1943, although some aircraft would continue to fly with them for several months.

355th Fighter Group

The 355th was one of the few groups that was constituted and activated on the same date — 12 November 1942. They began training on P-47s at Orlando Army Airfield, Florida, but moved to Richmond Army Air Force Base, Virginia on 17 February 1943. The Group was then transferred to the Philadelphia Municipal Airport on 4 March 1943 to continue training until orders were cut for overseas duty with the 8th Air Force on 16 June 1943. The Group sailed on the Queen Mary on 1 July 1943 and arrived in England five days later under the command Col William J. Cummings, Jr. The Group arrived at Steeple Morden on 8 July . The Group finally received enough fighters to fly their first full strength mission on 14 September when they conducted a fighter sweep to Belgium. Thereafter the 355th FG flew bomber escort missions to Berlin, Karlsruhe, Neuburg, Misburg, Glesenkirchen, and Minden, but was occasionally tasked to conduct fighter sweeps, patrols, and dive bombing missions. The Group flew its last P-47 mission on 13 March 1944 and then converted to the P-51.

While flying the Thunderbolt, the 355th had a total of 40 aerial victories, seven by the 354th, 17 by the 357th, 14 by the 358th, and two by the HQ Flight. The top scorer was Capt Norman B. Olson of the 357th with eight followed by Capt Walter J. Koraleski of the 354th with 2.33 kills and three 358th pilots — Maj Raymond B. Myers, 1Lt Harold H. Macurdy, and 1Lt James B. Dickson — with two each.

The 355th FG P-47s were camouflaged in the standard factory olive drab and neutral gray and carried 12-inch wide white cowl and tail bands with white spinners. Squadron codes were **WR** for the **354th**, **OS** for the **357th**, and **YF** for the **358th** Squadron.

(Above) Capt Walter Kossac of the 358th FS, 355th FG safely bellied in his P-47D-5-RE and walked away, but was later shot down on 7 November 1943. Coded YF*X, the serial number is believed to be 42-8455. The white cowl ring was a theater recognition marking to help differentiate the P-47 from the German Fw 190. (355th FG Association via R.E. Kuhnert)

(Below) *Lil Jo*, a P-47D-5-RE, was the mount of Lt Col Thomas 'Speed' Hubbard. Hubbard was the 355th FG's first executive Officer. Hubbard was shot down on 13 November 1943. *Lil Jo* carries a 108 gallon drop tank on the centerline rack and has a barely visible red surround around the fuselage insignia. (355th FG Association via R.E. Kuhnert)

356th Fighter Group

Authorization for the formation of the 356th Fighter Group was approved on 8 December 1942 with activation following four days later at Westover Field, Massachusetts. The Group conducted training at various bases within the United States (also known as the Zone of the Interior) before moving to England during August of 1943. The Group was temporarily housed at Goxhill until 5 October 1943 when they moved to Martlesham Heath — their base until the end of the war.

Lt Col Harold J. Rau commanded the Group until he was replaced by Col Einar A. Malstrom on 28 November. Malstrom led the Group until he was shot down and taken prisoner. Lt Col Philip B. Tukey, Jr. took command on 24 April 1944 and led the Group until he was replaced by Lt Col Donald A Baccus on 3 November 1944. Baccus led the 356th FG until it converted to P-51s.

The 356th FG's first combat mission was a fighter sweep on 15 October 1943. On 29 November the pilots broke the ice with five victories — the 359th FS scored three as (then) Major Don Baccus, Capt Ernest J. White Jr. and 2Lt James B. Smith each scored a single kill. The 361st FS's Lt Allen M. Metzger and the 360th FS's 1Lt Raymond B. Witherspoon also claimed an enemy aircraft. That all three squadrons scored their first victories on the same mission was a bit unusual and by an unusual contrast Capt John McNeill, one of the Group's flight leaders, flew an entire tour and even extended it, yet failed to encounter *any* enemy aircraft.

On 23 January 1944 the Group flew its first dive bombing mission — a strike on Gilze Rijen airfield in the Netherlands. The Group later supported OPERATION MARKET GARDEN, the airborne assault in the Netherlands, from 17 to 23 September 1944 and was awarded a DUC

P-47D-4-RA was flown by Lt Col John L. 'Moon' Elder, Jr., of the 357th FS, 355th FG. The aircraft is equipped with a Malcolm Hood for increased visibility from the cockpit. The white square around the R on the aft fuselage is another indicator that the aircraft has been designated 'War Weary' (aside from the normal 'WW' barely visible beneath the serial number on the tail). (Theo Bennett)

for its efforts. Probably the most unusual occurrence that the 356th FG experienced was when a pair of Thunderbolts shot up the 9th Air Force Headquarters at Lavay — over 200 miles away from their assigned target area. An anti-aircraft battery shot down one of the P-47s killing the pilot.

The 356th FG converted to P-51s during November of 1944.

The Group scored a total of 118 aerial kills while flying the Jug. The 361st FS led with 50, followed by the 360th FS with 40, and the 359th FS with 27. The HQ Flight claimed a single kill. Capt David F. Thwaites of the 361st FS became an ace with 6 kills. 1Lt Chester A. Vitale of the 360th had 4 enemy aircraft to his credit and seven pilots of the 359th FS each had a pair of victories.

The first P-47Ds were painted in the standard olive drab and neutral gray scheme applied to most USAAF fighters in the theater. The later P-47D-21s were received in a natural metal finish, but were given a green upper surface camouflage after arriving at Martlesham Heath. The white theater cowl bands and spinners were used on the early aircraft, but were later painted over with olive drab and neutral gray. Squadron codes were **OC** for the **359th**, **PI** for the **360th**, and **QI** for the **361st**.

Razorbacked P-47Ds of the 361st FS, 356th FG line up on their airfield. The second fighter, believed to be QI∗N, has a sharkmouth on the cowl — a rare marking for a P-47.

(Above) Lt Von Holyhausen of the 361st FS, 356th FG flew *China Doll* — a P-47D-6-RE (42-74679). White stars have been painted on the wheel covers. The fighter appears to have a semi-gloss — possibly waxed — paint finish. The P-47D-5 lacked the streamlined underwing bomb/drop tank racks commonly seen on later variants of the P-47D.

(Below) *MAD MARIAN*, a P-47D-20-RE of the 359th FS, 356th FG is parked among other Jugs at Goxhill sometime during the summer of 1944. Invasion stripes have been painted under the wings and fuselage. Invasion stripes gradually disappeared from the upper wing and fuselage surfaces shortly after D-Day.

(Below) The 360th FS, 356th FG flew a number of natural metal razorbacks. Among them was this P-47D-21-RE (PI*C/42-25534). No Group or Squadron markings have been applied to the aircraft. Natural metal P-47s usually wore black ID bands on the horizontal and vertical tail surfaces.

14

358th Fighter Group

The 358th Fighter Group was formed on 20 December 1942. Its first personnel were assigned to the unit on 1 January 1943 at Richmond Army Air Base where training began on Republic's heavyweight P-47. The Group moved to a number of locations along the US east coast before shipping out to England on 8 October 1943. The Group arrived in Liverpool on 20 October and settled in at Goxhill under the command of Col Cecil L. Wells. Like their nomadic life in the United States, the Group continued to move constantly while in Europe. The 358th FG went from Goxhill to Leiston, then to Raydon and High Halden before leaving the UK for France where they were based at Cretteville, Pontorson, Vitry-le-Francois, Mourmelon, and Toul. The unit then moved up to Sandhofen, Germany and finally back to Reims, France before returning to the US Zone of the Interior after the war.

The 358th FG served with both the 8th and 9th Air Forces. Their first 8th AF mission was flown on 20 December 1943 exactly one year after the Group was formed. The 8th AF then traded the 358th to the 9th Air Force for the 357th FG on 31 January 1944. The trade included an exchange of bases as well, further contributing to the 358th's nomadic life. While assigned to the 8th AF the Group flew 16 missions, the last occurring on 30 January. During this period they lost four P-47s while claiming only one enemy aircraft destroyed, five probables, and six damaged. The Group flew its first 9th AF mission on 3 February 1944.

The 358th FG was heavily involved in providing ground support for Allied ground forces after the Normandy invasion. A particularly productive day was 11 August 1944 when the Group flew eight missions destroying a railway gun and routing German troops in a forest near Redon. The Group followed up the next day with five missions attacking three trains, two motor convoys, and several pontoon bridges. On 28 September they dropped twenty-three 150 gallon napalm bombs on a fortified position near Metz, France and hit three other installations in the area.

The 358th was one of the few units to receive three DUCs. The first was for supporting the 7th Army from 24 December 1944 through 2 January 1945. The second DUC was awarded for action against the Germans trying to retreat across the Rhine River on 19-20 March. The third DUC came for their part in a series of devastating attacks on airfields in Munich, Ingolstadt, and other targets between 8 and 25 April 1945. The French Government awarded the 358th FG the Croix de Guerre with Palm for assisting in the liberation of France.

The Group claimed 106.5 enemy aircraft in the air. The 367th FS led with 50 kills, followed by the 365th with 27, the 366th with 25.5, and the Headquarters Flight with four. The top scoring pilots all had 3 victories including 1Lt Robert H. Rice and 1Lt Donald O. Scherer of the 366th, Capt James P. Schilke and F/O Jerrald P. Evoritt of the 367th, and Col Cecil L. Wells of the HQ Flight. Five pilots in the 365th had two kills each.

The Jugs were painted in olive drab and neutral gray — a scheme carried over to the 9th AF after the unit was transferred. Squadron codes were **CH** for the **365th**, **IA** for the **366th** and **CP** for the **367th**. The 358th FG used no group markings while assigned to the 8th AF. When the 358th FG was assigned to the First Tactical Air Force during November of 1944 the tails of their Jugs were painted orange and their cowl rings and prop hubs were painted red. During early 1945 the cowlings were painted in the squadron colors — yellow for the 366th, white for the 367th, and red for the 367th. Individual aircraft often carried personal markings.

(Right) Thunderbolts of the 368th FS, 359th FG line up to display a common theme — all are named after characters in Al Capp's Li'l Abner comic strip. Left to right are *LI'L ABNER, MAMMY YOKUM, DAISY MAE, PAPPY YOKUM,* and *MARRYIN' SAM.*

359th Fighter Group

The 359th FG was formed on 20 December 1942 and activated on 15 January 1943. The first personnel were not actually assigned until early March of 1943. The unit moved from Westover Field, Massachusetts to Grenier Field, New Hampshire, and then to Farmingdale Army Air Base, New York — the home of Republic Aviation — where they began training on P-47s under Col Avelin P. Tacon, Jr. When ordered overseas, the men were put on three different transports. The crossing was uneventful and while they all arrived on 19 October, the men debarked at three different ports — Liverpool, Glasgow, and Gourock, Scotland. Troop trains carried them to Station 133, Wretham that same day.

The Group went into action with a fighter sweep over northern France on 13 December 1943. Seven sweeps were flown that month and in 1944 they continued flying escort, patrol, dive bombing, strafing, and weather reconnaissance missions. After a little less than five months of combat operations with the P-47s, the Group converted to the P-51.

The Group claimed 42 enemy aircraft shot down — 19 by the 370th FS, 15 by the 369th FS, and six by the 368th FS — while flying the P-47. The HQ Flight picked up two more. The top scorers were 1Lt Ray S. Wetmore of the 370th FS with 4.25 kills, 1Lt Robert J. Booth of the 369th with four, and Lt Col Albert R. Tyrell of the 368th with two. All of these pilots eventually became aces and Wetmore, with 24.5 victories, became the leading ace in the ETO still on flying status.

The first P-47Ds wore the standard olive drab and neutral gray scheme, but later P-47D-21s were flown in a natural metal finish. During March of 1944 a bright green 24-inch wide cowl band was applied as a Group marking. Squadron codes were **CV** for the **368th**, **IV** for the **369th**, and **CR** for the **370th** Squadron.

(Above) *Mary* was a P-47D-5-RE assigned to the 369th FS, 359th FG during the summer of 1944. *Mary* still wears the remnants of her invasion stripes under the aft fuselage and has oversized US insignia under the wings. The old style US insignia has been painted on the wheel covers. The canopy frame is believed to be white, but may be natural metal.

361st Fighter Group

The 361st FG was formed on 28 January 1943 with personnel being assigned on 10 February at Richmond Army Air Base, Virginia under the command of Col Thomas J. J. Christian, Jr. The Group trained with P-47s at Langley Field, Virginia, Millville Army Air Field, New Jersey, Camp Springs Army Air Field, Maryland and then back to Virginia before shipping out to join the 8th Air Force in England. The Group arrived in England on 29 November and settled down at Bottisham — the last Thunderbolt group to join the 8th AF.

They flew their first mission on 21 January 1944. The unit served primarily as a bomber escort group over the Continent, but was also actively engaged in Big Week 20 to 25 February 1944 — a period in which the USAAF attacked the Luftwaffe in full force, seeking it out from its airfields to its factories. The 361st later engaged in counter air patrols, fighter sweeps, and strafing and dive bombing missions. The Group converted to the P-51 Mustang during May of 1944.

The 361st FG was credited with 34 air-to-air victories while flying the Jug. Three pilots, Capt Robert E. Sedman of the 374th and Maj George L. Merritt, Jr. and 2Lt Alton B. Snyder, both of the 375th, all had three victories to their credit.

The Group's P-47Ds were camouflaged with olive drab and neutral gray, however, the later P-47D-21s were left in a natural metal finish. Twenty-four inch yellow cowl ring bands were applied in March of 1944 as a Group ID marking. The squadron codes were B7 for the **374th**, E2 for the **375th**, and E9 for the **376th**.

5th Emergency Rescue Squadron

The 5th Emergency Rescue Squadron was formed as a detachment of the 65th Fighter Wing in May of 1944, but was redesignated and activated as the 5th Air Sea Rescue Squadron on 26 January 1945. The unit was originally under the command of an ex-56th FG pilot, Major Robert P. Gerhart, until he was replaced by Maj E. L. Larson during January of 1945. The 5th ERS was initially based at Boxted, but moved to Halesworth during January of 1945.

The Squadron flew P-47D-5s and D-21s most of which were classified as 'WW' (War Weary) and no longer considered suitable for combat operations. The 5th flew its first rescue mission on 10 May 1944 and eventually flew a total of 3,481 sorties while losing only one Thunderbolt on 1 August 1944. The unit scored no victories against manned aircraft, although the aircraft were fully armed for self-protection. The weapons came in handy on 30 June 1944 when Lt J. Tucker shot down a V 1 Buzz Bomb over the English Channel. It was the first V 1 destroyed by the 8th Air Force.

In the ASR configuration the T-Bolts carried a 150 gallon belly tank, four smoke markers, usually carried on the lower centerline behind the drop tank, and an M-Type dinghy pack under each wing. The dinghy packs were dropped to airmen in the water, while the smoke markers allowed air-sea rescue launches based on the coast to locate the downed airmen. Since the P-47s were all 'War-Wearys' they were in their standard olive drab and neutral gray camouflage finishes, although at least one aircraft was in a natural metal finish and it was the one lost on 1 August 1944. The cowls had distinctive 15-inch wide red, white, and blue bands. The wing tips were painted yellow and yellow bands were carried on all of the tail surfaces. The **5th Emergency Rescue Squadron's** code was **5F**.

Contrary Mary, a P-47D-11-RE (42-75221), was flown by Capt John W. Guckeyson of the 375th FS, 361st FG. Guckeyson scored 2.5 kills during 1944. A single 108 gallon fuel tank is carried on the centerline rack. (Steve Gotes Collection)

Maj Roy B. Caviness brought *Goona* home despite having his hydraulic system shot up. *Goona* was a P-47D-4-RA (42-22784) assigned to the 376th FS, 361st FG. Caviness commanded both the 361st and 78th Fighter Groups during 1944 and 1945. (Steve Gotes Collection)

495th Fighter Training Group

The 495th Fighter Training Group began as the 6th Pursuit Wing on 19 October 1940. It was activated on 18 December 1940, but deactivated on 7 December 1941. It was reactivated as the 6th Fighter Wing on 7 June 1942 and was sent to join the 8th AF during August of 1942. It was assigned

the task of training replacement pilots, but was disbanded on 13 September 1942 after it had been redesignated the 2906th Observation Training Group. The unit was rebuilt as the 495th FTG on 25 December to train P-47 pilots for both the 8th and 9th Air Forces. Col Jack W. Hickman was appointed Group Commander and his two subordinate squadrons, the 551st and 552nd, were equipped with P-47Cs and Ds. The Group was based at Atcham, England until 15 February 1945 when it was moved to Cheddington. The Group trained new pilots in tactics, formation flying, gunnery, strafing, and dive bombing. The P-47s were painted in the standard olive drab and gray, although a few were later left in natural metal. Squadron codes were **DQ** for the **551st** and **VM** for the **552nd**.

3rd Gunnery and Tow Target Flight

The flight was based at East Wretham with the 359th Fighter Group and flew P-47Ds towing target sleeves for gunnery practice. The flight did not carry any special markings or aircraft codes.

65th Fighter Wing Headquarters Flight

The 65th was originally constituted as the 4th Air Defense Wing on 25 March 1943 and activated two days later. The unit moved to England during June of 1943 for duty with the 8th AF and was redesignated the 65th Fighter Wing during July of 1943. Col Jesse Auton was the first commander. The Flight was equipped with the P-47C, D, and M during the course of the war. The aircraft were left in a natural metal finish. The aircraft served as transports for staff officers to visit other groups, staff meetings, and to maintain flying proficiency. The aircraft carried the code letters **JA** — perhaps not so coincidentally the initials of Col Auton. The aircraft carried a variety of red and white markings including a red and white spiraled spinner and a 24-inch white band around the cowl.

66th Fighter Wing Headquarters Flight

The 5th Air Defense Wing was constituted on 25 March 1943 and activated on 27 March. It moved to Duxford, England during May of 1943 to join the 8th AF. It was redesignated the 66th Fighter Wing in July. BGen Murray C. Woodbury was the first commander. The unit's duties were identical to the 65th FW HQ Flight. Its P-47Ds were left in a natural metal finish and had yellow, blue, white, and red checkers on the cowl. The Flight's aircraft did not carry code letters.

The 5th Emergency Rescue Squadron used 'war weary' P-47s in the air-sea rescue role. *Miss Margaret* (5F*E/42-8693) has her yellow, black, and white nose art emblazoned on the red, white, and blue cowl. Many 5th ERS P-47s carried yellow tail bands and wing tips as well.

These two P-47Ds apparently taxied into each other — demonstrating that if Republic could build it, somewhere out there was a lieutenant that could bend it. The 495th FG was a training group, consequently accidents were not unknown. The twisted fuselage of BQ*P probably meant the aircraft was a writeoff. (Fred C. Dickey)

Col Jesse Auton of the 65th FW HQ Flight carried the code J*A on his 'War Weary' P-47D-22-RE. The 65th FW HQ Flight flew War Weary aircraft for use as fast transports, liaison aircraft, and to maintain flying proficiency. Although 'War Weary', the P-47 appears to be kept in excellent condition. (Garry Fry)

The 9th Air Force

The 9th Air Force began as V Air Support Command when it was authorized on 21 August 1941 and activated on 1 September. The unit became the 9th Air Force during April of 1942 and was ordered to Egypt where it began combat operations on 12 November 1942. The 9th AF and its subordinate units supported the Allied drive across Egypt and Libya, the Tunisian Campaign, and the later invasions of Sicily and southern Italy. It was then ordered to England where it became the Tactical Air Force for the invasion of France. The 9th AF provided support for pre-D-Day operations and thereafter was extensively involved in providing tactical support to the beachhead. The 9th AF later provided continual support in the drives across France and into Germany.

The 9th AF could easily be called the 'Thunderbolt Air Force' since it had more assigned P-47 Groups than any other numbered Air Force during WW II. Due to its rugged construction the P-47 was an ideal aircraft to fill the tactical role — the forte of the 9th Air Force. The lethal fire power of eight .50 caliber machine guns made it perfectly suited for low-level strafing. Additionally, it was capable of carrying bombs in the dive bomber role and rockets for low-level attacks on trains, armor, and other vehicles. Its ability to absorb battle damage and continue to fight (and get its pilot home) was a large plus. Although low-level tactical work was always dangerous and often unglamorous, the Jug played the role to the hilt.

The 9th AF must be given a large amount of the credit for the Allied success in winning the ground war against the German Army. Their near continuous presence over the battlefield and over the German's rear areas kept the Wehrmacht off balance by denying them essential supplies, cutting communications, ground, and rail transportation, and attacking concentrations of troops, armor, and fuel and ammo dumps.

General Hoyt Vandenberg, the 9th AF commander, pointed out that the fighter-bombers, seldom met German aircraft and had little opportunity to run up high aerial victory scores, yet their job "...is just as exacting as that of high scoring aces". During December of 1944 the 9th AF Command sent a memo to all Groups to submit the names of their best pilots in nine different categories. Maj Frank H. Peppers of the 362nd FG was named the best of the fighter-bomber pilots in the 9th and also the champion bridge-buster with fifteen bridges — both single and double track railway spans — during his 24-month tour of duty. Capt Irving I. Ostuw of the 368th FG's 'Thunder-Bums' knocked down 75 buildings in enemy held areas. Capt Carroll A. Peterson, assigned to the 362nd FG, silenced 75 gun emplacements, but was later killed in action. Capt Wilfred B. Crutchfield, another 362nd FG pilot, was the champion railroad car destroyer with 350 to his credit. Capt Kent C. Geyer, another 362nd FG pilot, received credit for 80 railroad track cuts. Capt Francis

P. McIntire was tops at sealing tunnels with six closed off to the Germans. From the 368th FG came the top motor transport destroyer, 1Lt Henry B. Hamilton, who littered northwestern Europe with 300 destroyed vehicles. Rounding out the best-of-the-best was 1Lt William J. Garry of the 368th FG — a specialist at taking out tanks and armored vehicles with a score of 32 destroyed.

Since most of the fighter groups in the 9th AF were engaged in the same tactical target areas their missions at times overlapped. For the most part the missions and incidents covered in the histories of the various groups, while unique to the individual group, present a fair representation of the entire 9th Air Force's roster of Thunderbolts.

From 25 March through 8 May 1945 Ninth AF P-47s flew 29,216 sorties, claimed 240 aerial kills, 16 probables, and 98 damaged. The 9th produced at least 12 aces that scored all or a portion of their victories while flying the P-47.

36th Fighter Group

The 36th Fighter Group was originally formed as the 36th Pursuit Group and equipped with Curtiss P-36s when activated at Langley Field, Virginia on 1 February 1940. The Group was transferred to Losey Field, Puerto Rico and re-equipped with Bell P-39s and Curtiss P-40s on 2 January 1941. The 36th PG flew anti-submarine patrols while serving as part of the Caribbean and Panama Canal Defense Force. The Group was redesignated the 36th Fighter Group during May of 1942 and recalled to Morrison Field, Florida to train with Republic P-47 Thunderbolts. The 36th FG moved to various bases around the US until it was considered combat ready and sent to England during April of 1944. The Group consisted of the 22nd, 23rd, 32nd, 36th, and 53rd Fighter Squadrons. The 32nd and 36th FSs were reassigned to other units before the Group went into combat. The 36th flew its first mission on 8 May 1944 while commanded by Lt Col Van H. Slayden.

Initial operations included armed reconnaissance, escort, and interdiction missions such as strafing and dive bombing armored vehicles, bridges, trains, gun emplacements, troop concentrations, communication centers, air fields and other targets of value. All of these strikes were part of the softening up process during the weeks prior to D-Day. On D-Day, 6 June 1944, the 36th FG patrolled the airspace over the beaches and flew close support missions. During July the Group moved to Bruncheville, France and became what could be dubbed a 'Flying Circus' because they operated from (and lived in) a constant state of mobility, under canvas, and always ready to move up in the wake of the advancing ground forces. The entire unit was capable of packing up and moving to a new location in a matter of hours.

During August of 1944 they moved to Le Mans to support General Patton's Third Army. On 2 August the 36th FG caught an ammunition

DOOGAN, a P-47D-22-RE of the 22nd FS, 36th FG, taxis down a snow packed runway on Christmas Eve 1944 at Le Coulet, Belgium. The cowl ring has been painted red — the squadron color. The canopy frames are believed to be red as well. (L. Davis via J. Lansdale)

MAJ MAC, a P-47D-28-RA of the 23rd FS, 36th FG, was the mount of Lt L. W. Magnuson. The back half of the cowl and the entire tail are painted yellow. The front half of the cowl is painted red. (Don Madden)

train and blew it up at Noyon and surprised another at Appilly and destroyed it as well. They then found an oil train and set it ablaze. Numerous supply barges were strafed and burned on the Oise Canal.

On 7 August the Group hit the marshaling yards at Chartres, burning 85 to 100 railroad cars. A change of pace on 12 August found eight P-47s attacking eight German destroyers trying to break out of Lorient harbor. One destroyer was set on fire while the others were damaged. On 25 August the 36th destroyed five locomotives and forty rail cars. The cycle was repeated throughout the month as the 36th FG deprived the Germans of supplies that were desperately needed to halt Patton's army as it swept across France.

On 1 September the 36th FG caught columns of retreating Germans south of the Loire River near Clamecy and destroyed 500 German vehicles. The feat resulted in a DUC for the Group. The Group moved forward to Athis, France during September and on to Le Coulet, Belgium on 23 October to support the Ninth Army. The Group took part in the Battle of the Bulge from December of 1944 through January of 1945 flying close support and armed reconnaissance missions. During February of 1945 they helped the First Army's advance across the Roer River and supported operations at the Remagen bridge head. The Group took a heavy toll of German railroad rolling stock on 22 January when seven locomotives and 282 rail cars were destroyed and another 125 damaged. An additional 17 installations were struck on 22 January, but two P-47s were lost and eight more damaged.

During March of 1945 the Group provided cover for the Allied airborne assault across the Rhine. On 13 March the 53rd FS caught a formation of Me 109s near the Remagen Bridge and shot down five and damaged two more. The German fighters were also forced to prematurely salvo their bombs. On 14 March two squadrons of the 36th FG caught approximately 50 Ju 87 Stukas armed and ready for take off at Lippe

airfield. Several bombing and strafing passes resulted in 23 Ju 87s and one Me 109 destroyed and another 20 Stukas damaged. Later that day the 23rd FS added eight more Stukas and three Me 109s to the total while damaging another six Ju 87s. The 22nd FS accounted for two Fw 190s and damaged an Me 109. One P-47 failed to return from this mission.

Lt Col Paul P. Douglas assumed command of the 36th FG during April of 1945. On 12 April the Group earned its second DUC when it set a record for the number of enemy aircraft destroyed on the ground in a single day. At Schkeuditz they destroyed three Do 217s, 14 He 111s, and a hangar. At Leipzig/Mockau they added seven Me 109s, an Me 262 jet fighter, five Me 410s, nine Fw 190s, 16 Ju 88s, a Ju 87, 10 trainers and a captured P-47. Claims for the day were 73 destroyed and 27 damaged against four P-47s damaged by flak. They accomplished this feat using only eleven P-47s. In addition to its two DUCs, the Group was also awarded the Belgian Fourragere and was cited in the Belgian Army Order of the Day. The last mission of the war was flown on 8 May 1945.

The Group had 33 confirmed kills — the 22nd FS with four, the 23rd FS with 10, and the 53rd FS with 19. The top scorer was Maj John L. Wright with three kills.

The Group's P-47s were generally left in natural metal — a common condition for USAAF fighters during the latter half of 1944 and all of 1945. The several variations of Group markings on the tail ranged from the tail surfaces being painted overall yellow to yellow fin tips or yellow rudders. The squadrons also went through a number of cowl color changes ranging from solid colored cowls to an 18-inch band around the center of the cowling to a colored nose ring. The 22nd FS used red, the 23rd wore yellow, and the 53rd FS used blue. Aircraft code letters were **3T** for the **22nd**, **7U** for the **23rd**, and **6V** for the **53rd**.

(Above) Lt Don Madden of the 23rd FS, 36th FG flew *DIXIE*, a P-47D-26-RA. *EASY'S ANGELS* painted on the vertical tail surfaces refers to squadron commander Maj 'Easy' Miles. The marking appeared on most of the 23rd FS's aircraft near the end of the war. (Don Madden)

(Below) 6V*J was a P-47D-30-RA assigned to the 53rd FS, 36th FG at Le Coulet, Belgium during the fall of 1944. The tail surfaces are painted yellow — the Group marking — while the cowl is painted blue — the 53rd's squadron color. (J. V. Crow)

48th Fighter Group

The 48th FG was originally formed as a light bombardment group on 20 November 1940, but was not activated until 15 January 1941. During September of 1942 it was redesignated a dive bomber group, but later became the 48th Fighter Group during August of 1943. During this period the Group flew A-20s, B-18s, A-24s, A-31s, A-35s, A-36s, P-39s, and P-40s. Four squadrons, the 492nd, 493rd, 494th, and 495th Fighter Squadrons, were assigned to the Group, but before being sent overseas to join the 9th AF, in keeping with the policy of three squadrons per group, the 495th FS was dropped. After arriving at Ibssley, England during March of 1944 the 48th began training on the P-47. Their first mission, a fighter sweep, was flown on 20 April 1944. Col George L. Wertenbaker, Jr. assumed command on 23 April. Dive bombing and escort missions were flown prior to D-Day and on 6 June the Group struck artillery emplacements and bridges. For the remainder of the Normandy Campaign, they flew additional tactical missions cutting rail lines, blowing up fuel dumps, trains, and disrupting German transportation

The 48th FG moved to Deux Jumeaux, France on 18 June 1944 and helped the Allied forces during the break through at St Lo during July and their close support operations continued during the drive across France in August. The Group flew support missions during the Airborne attack on Holland during September. The Group received a Belgian government citation for this action. During this period the Group had been on the move first to Villacoubly in August, to Cambrai/Niergnies in September, and then to St Tronde, Belgium.

On 15 October the 48th FG flew nine squadron strength sorties attacking gun positions, troops, and buildings in support of XIX Corps. The 492nd FS was returning to base on one of these sorties when they were ordered to disperse a counter attack by thirty German tanks. Despite being low on fuel and with only two bombs left the 492nd went in at minimum altitude in the face of heavy ground fire and made two strafing attacks. When forced to break off due to low fuel the German Panzers were in full retreat leaving their dead and wounded behind. The 492nd FS was awarded a DUC for this action. A second DUC resulted from a coordinated air-ground support mission with the US 9th Army on 6 December 1944. Due to a low cloud base this mission was conducted at minimum altitude over the entire target area. Again, in the face of heavy small arms fire and flak the 48th FG destroyed troop concentrations, ground entrenchments, and fortified buildings. Several P-47s were damaged during the strafing runs, but after the Group left the 9th Army made a rapid and almost unopposed advance through the area.

On Washington's birthday, 22 February 1945, three Me 262 pilots apparently decided to have some fun at the expense of some 493rd FS Jugs by bouncing them. For some unexplained reason the German jets held their fire and tried to pull away straight and level. Despite the surprise the 493rd FS pilots fired a couple of snap bursts and damaged two of the Me 262s.

The Group found itself making an all-out effort on 18 April 1945 and sent 110 Thunderbolts on six missions to strafe Luftwaffe airfields at Grossenheim, Oschatz, and other targets of opportunity. The 48th claimed three aircraft, four locomotives, 50 freight cars, 28 vehicles, four warehouses, a supply depot, 20 horse-drawn carts, and a building housing German troops. On 8 May 1945 the 48th Fighter Group flew its last mission of the war.

The Group was credited with 18.5 victories, three for the 492nd, 9.5 for the 493rd, and six for the 494th. The top scorer was 2Lt Gordon P. Humphries with 1.5 victories followed by 2Lt William G. Dilley, Jr. with 1.25 kills.

The 48th FG's P-47s were usually left in the delivery scheme of natural metal. From late 1944 the P-47s carried a red and white checked cowl with the cowl ring and rudder painted in the squadron color — red for

Lt J. P. Crow said farewell to *Sweet Louise* on a field outside of Paris during June of 1945. This colorful razorback Jug was a P-47D-22-RE of the 492nd FS, 48th FG. (J. P. Crow)

I7*E, a P-47-D-28-RA of the 493rd FS, 48th FG suffered heavy damage during a wheels up landing during the spring of 1945. The red and white checks on the cowl are a group marking and are unusual in that most 9th AF fighter groups carried the group marking on the tail. The cowl ring and rudder are blue. (W. N. Hess)

the 492nd, blue for the 493rd, and yellow for the 494th. Squadron codes consisted of **F4** for the **492nd**, **I7** for the **493rd**, and **6M** for the **494th**.

While stationed in Germany the Group started to receive new P-47Ns although they were never used in combat. These P-47s had compressibility flaps which Lt John P. Crow decided to test by climbing to 35,000 feet, doing a split-S, and diving at full throttle. His air speed indicator hit the 550 mph peg. As condensation on the windscreen blocked his visibility, he eased back on the throttle while the heavy fighter shook and shuddered. Using all of his strength he hauled back on the stick and, at 20,000 feet, flipped open the compressibility flaps and blacked out. He regained consciousness at 18,000 feet while on his back. Crow rolled over and returned to base. The flaps worked — although he could have just as easily been a big smoking hole in the ground... .

50th Fighter Group

The 50th FG was organized as the 50th Pursuit Group on 20 November 1940 and activated on 15 January 1941. It was redesignated the 50th Fighter Group during May of 1942 and served as a part of the Fighter Command School where it tested equipment and trained air defense units. The Group transferred to the School of Applied Tactics where it trained pilots in fighter tactics under simulated combat conditions. The 50th used a large variety of aircraft including P-40s, P-47s, DB-7s, P-51s, and P-70s.

The 50th FG was fully equipped with P-47s when it was assigned to the 9th AF and sent to Lymington, England during April of 1944. It began combat operations on 1 May 1944 flying the mandatory fighter sweep over France and was thereafter used on escort and dive bombing missions for the rest of the month. The Group flew air cover missions over the Normandy beaches on 6 and 7 June and was moved to Carentan, France on 25 June where it began a nomadic lifestyle — moving to Meautis in August, to Orly on 4 September, Laon on 15 September, and the Lyons/Bron area on 28 September.

During July the 50th blasted targets in the St. Lo area in support of the Allied breakout. During August the 50th was called upon to provide fighter cover for the British battleship HMS *Warspite*. The old battleship was lobbing salvos of 15-inch armor piercing shells onto Ile de Cezembre off the coast of France. The island's German garrison had continued to hold out after the port city of St. Malo had surrendered.

The 50th continued to fly close support and interdiction missions through the month of September. On 13 September a flight of Thunderbolts strafed and destroyed 11 enemy aircraft on the ground at Seligerstadt. Two days later the 81st FS was bounced by 12 Fw 190s. Five of the Focke Wulfs were shot down without loss. 1Lts Warren E. Foote and Hugh Hall each

1Lt Kenneth T. Jones' *EVELYN*, **a razorback P-47D (6M*Z) was downed over Normandy during June of 1944. The evenly bent propeller blades indicate the Curtiss Electric propeller was still turning when Jones set the Jug down. Lt Jones was assigned to the 494th FS, 48th FG and scored a lone kill on 27 December 1944 while flying a different aircraft. (P. W. Robinson)**

This unmarked P-47D, believed to be a replacement aircraft, is rearmed at St Trond, Belgium during the fall of 1944. Multiple sorties and quick turnarounds were the order of the day for 9th AF Thunderbolts. (J. P. Crow)

Lt Robert M. Harding of the 10th FS, 50th FG flew *Miz Frankie*, **a P-47D-27-RE (T5*Z).** *Miz Frankie* **retains her invasion stripes under the aft fuselage. (R. M. Harding)**

bagged a pair of the German fighters.

During early January of 1945 the Group helped stem the German offensive in the Saar-Hardt area. This was an offensive designed to shift Allied pressure away from German forces attempting to withdraw from the Battle of the Bulge. The Group also took part in the air offensive that reduced the Colmar bridgehead.

On 23 February 1945 Lt Gilbert Burns took off on a mission over Landou, Germany. Flying at 300 feet he went after a pile of ammo crates in a valley near a rail line. His P-47 was hit by flak which disabled both the rudder pedals and the control column and the cockpit filled with smoke. Jettisoning the canopy he saw that he was too low to bail out. His Jug was doing about 260 mph, but flying straight into Germany. Burns used his trim tabs to correct the aircraft when his left wing started to dip. By continually adjusting the tabs Burns was able to make a broad shallow turn and head for home. The damaged fighter began to shudder at 255 mph, so he guessed that it would stall out at 250

P-47s of the 50th FG taxi out for a mission on or shortly after D-Day — the Allied invasion of Normandy. *Gertie* was assigned to the Group's 313th FS. (J. V. Crow)

(Below) Maj Glenn T. Eagleston flew this P-47D-30-RE (FT*L/44-20473) while in France during early 1945. Eagleston was assigned to the 353rd FS, 354th FG and was the top 9th AF ace with 18.5 victories. The black winged skull and cowl flaps over a yellow cowl were a squadron marking while the eagle on the fuselage was Eagleston's personal marking. (USAF)

mph. He eased off on the throttle to slowly lose altitude and avoid a stall and finally made a crash landing alongside his runway. Burns walked away from the fighter without a scratch — or any additional major damage to the P-47.

During March of 1945 the Group supported the drive that breached the Siegfried Line and allowed the Allies to move into Germany. The 50th received its first DUC for close cooperation with the US 7th Army. The Group isolated the battle area by cutting communications and bridges and destroying ammunition dumps and supply warehouses. A second DUC followed on 25 April 1945 when the Group destroyed numerous enemy aircraft on an airfield near Munich. The Group flew its last combat mission in May of 1945.

The Group was credited with 51 victories — the 10th FS claiming 11, the 81st FS claiming 26, and the 313th FS accounting for 14. Lt Col Robert D. Johnson was the top scorer and lone ace with six kills.

The 50th FG aircraft flew with natural metal schemes. All three squadrons carried a Group marking consisting of a red cowl ring and a red band on the fin and rudder (and possibly the horizontal tail surfaces as well), but this is believed to be related to the Group's service with the 1st Tactical Air Force — a provisional unit based on the continent and tasked with providing the ground forces with rapid reaction close air support. The **10th FS** was assigned the code **5T**, the **81st** received **2N**, and the **313th** was given **W3**.

354th Fighter Group

The 354th FG came into being after Pearl Harbor. It was constituted on 12 November 1942 and activated on 15 November. While training with P-39s the Group served as part of the West Coast Air Defense Command. Orders were cut on 4 November 1943 sending the Group to the United Kingdom where it was based at Greenham Common and equipped with P-51s. It became known as the pioneer Mustang Group.

The Mustangs were replaced by P-47s from November of 1944 through February of 1945. The conversion came just in time for the Group to help counter the German's offensive during the Battle of the Bulge. The Group supported the Allied ground forces by destroying tanks, troop concentrations, and gun positions and interdicting enemy supplies by strafing the roads and rail lines. While based at Orconte and Muerthe-et-Moselle, France two of the 354th FG aces, Maj James B. Dalglish and Capt Kenneth H. Dahlberg, each added a pair of enemy aircraft to their score.

While flying the Thunderbolt the 353rd Squadron was credited with 15 kills, the 355th with nine, and the 356th with five for a Group total of 29 aerial victories Maj Glenn T. Eagleston of the 353rd FS was the 9th AF's top ace with 18.5 kills. The Group was awarded the French Croix de Guerre with Palm for their efforts during the period from 1 December to 31 December 1944.

Despite the fact that the Group flew the P-47 for only a short period of time, they managed to create some interesting, if short-lived, unit markings. The 353rd FS started with blue triangles on the cowl flaps and a 12-inch blue band around the center of the cowl. Later, the entire cowl was painted yellow and the flaps black. A few aircraft carried a winged black skull and bones on the cowl. The 355th FS featured light blue cowls and cowl flaps with a white band in the center of the cowl. Two rows of light blue diamonds were superimposed on the white cowl band.

The 356th FS carried all white cowls and cowl flaps with a 24-inch blue band around the center. Ten white stars were painted on the blue band. All of the squadrons carried a black ID band on the fin and rudder. Squadron codes were **FT** for the **353rd**, **GQ** for the **355th**, and **AJ** for the **356th**.

358th Fighter Group

The 358th Fighter Group was created on 20 December 1942. It went on active duty on 1 January 1943 equipped with P-47s. The Group moved overseas on 20 October 1943 and was stationed at Goxhill, England as part of the 8th AF. On 31 January 1944 the Group was reassigned to the 9th AF. The Group went through a number of station changes moving to Leiston, Raydon, and High Halden, England until 13 April 1944 when the Group moved to A-5 at Crettville, France on 7 June 1944. Additional moves to Pontorson, Vitry Le Francois, Mourmelon, and Toul followed as the Allied ground forces advanced. The 358th FG was temporarily transferred to the 1st Tactical Air Force on 1 November 1944, but remained administratively with the 9th AF until VE-Day.

Lt Raymond P. Bain of the 355th FS, 354th FG originally had his P-47D named *Scatterbrain* — a name suggested by his girlfriend Mary who liked the song 'Scatterbrain'. Bain's crew chief changed the name to *Scatter Bain* after the Lieutenant brought the fighter back from Bastogne shot full of holes. (R. P. Bain)

CH*K, a natural metal P-47D-28-RA of the 365th FS, 358th FG, was colorfully marked with a red spinner and cowl ring, a white cowl, black and white checked cowl flaps, and a bright orange tail. The Group was known as the 'Orangetails'. (P. Stein)

The 358th FG began operations with the 9th AF under the command of Col Cecil L. Wells. Most of the operations consisted of the standard 9th AF role of supporting the ground forces. A mission flown on 1 August 1944 was probably the most unusual mission of all when the Group was tasked to strike some hay wagons. The hay wagons were carrying concealed AA weapons.

On 20 September the Group lost Col Wells in an accident. His Thunderbolt took a flak hit which knocked out the controls and he was forced to bail out. His parachute deployed and he landed near a Medic unit, but when the Medics reached him they found Wells dead. Apparently he had hit the tail plane which caused a fatal injury. Col James B. Tipton took

command on 22 September and led the Group until he was relieved by Col John M. Thacker. Thacker served until the war's end.

The Group earned three DUCs and the French Croix de Guerre with Palm. The first DUC was awarded for the destruction of 27 enemy aircraft during the period of 24 December 1944 through 1 January 1945. The 365th Squadron was credited with eight enemy aircraft, the 367th with 13, and the 366th with six — all scored on 1 January 1945. The second DUC was earned during actions on 19 and 20 March 1945. The Group pounded German forces trying to flee from the area west of the Rhine River by destroying large numbers of motor transports. The third DUC was awarded for strikes on airfields near Munich and Ingolstadt from 8 through the 25 April 1945. The 366th FS had four aerial victories, while the 367th FS scored nine kills. During this period they continued to support the US 7th Army as it advanced across northwestern Europe. The French Croix de Guerre with Palm came for their role in the liberation of France.

On 2 April 1945 the 358th FG was based on German soil at Sandhofen where it ended the war. The Group's final victory total was 101.99 kills. The 367th FS led with 49.49 victories, the 365th followed with 27, while the 366th had 25.5. Five pilots tied for top gun with three victories each — 1Lt R. H. Rice (366th), 1Lt W. E. Owens, 1Lt J. F. Schilke, Capt A. W. Perry, and Capt R. E. Ward — all with the 367th FS.

(Below) *Stinky* was flown by Lt Leo D. Volkmer of the 365th FS, 358th FG during the spring of 1945. Volkmer and *Stinky*, a P-47D-30-RA, scored a pair of victories on 30 April 1945. The war ended eight days later. (L. D. Volkmer)

A ground crewman guides a P-47D-10-RE of the 366th FS, 358th FG as it taxis out to main runway at Raydon, England. The Jug retains its olive drab and neutral gray camouflage which is thoroughly compromised by the orange tail and red and yellow cowl.

TARHEEL HAL was one of the gaudiest P-47s in the 9th AF. The colorful Jug was flown by Lt 'Ike' Davis of the 366th FS, 358th FG. The P-47D-30-RA's (IA*N) cowl was red and yellow, the forward fuselage was blue with white stars and red trim, and the tail surfaces were orange. The cowl flaps were red, white, and blue with white stars — a motif repeated on the rudder trim tab. (P. Stein)

While assigned to the 9th AF, the 358th Fighter Group apparently did not use any unique markings. When they joined the 1st TAF during November of 1944 they painted the entire tail orange which earned them the name 'The Orangetails'. The propeller hubs and cowl rings were painted red, the 1st TAF identification color. Later, the rest of the cowls were painted in squadron colors — white for the 365th FS, yellow for the 366th, and red for the 367th. Some cowl flaps also carried various designs. The **365th FS** wore the code **CH**, **366th** was assigned **IA**, and the **367th FS** was given **CP**. The codes were painted black on the natural metal aircraft.

(Above) White kicking mules adorn the red cowl flaps of this orange-tailed 367th FS, 358th FG P-47D-28-RE. Unfortunately CP*J's cowl logo was not readable in the original print. (Author's Collection)

(Below) CP*D, a P-47D-20-RE of the 367th FS, 358th FG, suffered extensive flak damage to its port wing and fuselage. Fire fighters pour foam on spilled fuel to prevent a fire while a medic attends to the pilot in the cockpit. (Author's Collection)

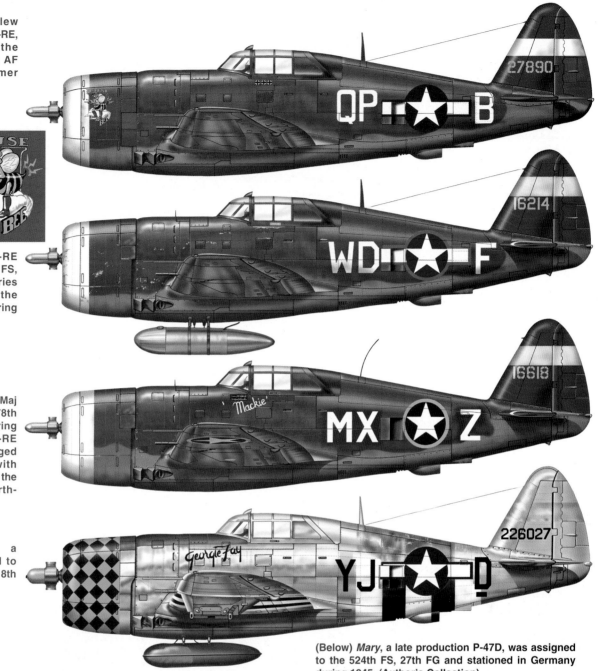

Maj Duane Beeson flew *BOISE BEE*, a P-47D-1-RE, while assigned to the 334th FS, 4th FG, 8th AF during the late summer and fall of 1943.

WD*F was a P-47C-2-RE assigned to the 335th FS, 4th FG, 8th AF. It carries the US insignia with the red surround used during the summer of 1943.

'Mackie' was flown by Maj Harry Dayhuff of the 78th FG during the late spring of 1943. The P-47C-2-RE carried the yellow ringed insignia associated with OPERATION TORCH — the Allied landings in north-west Africa.

Georgie Fay was a P-47D-22-RE assigned to the 351st FS, 353rd FG, 8th AF.

(Below) *Mary*, a late production P-47D, was assigned to the 524th FS, 27th FG and stationed in Germany during 1945. (Author's Collection)

362nd Fighter Group

The 362nd FG was formed on 11 February 1943 and activated on 1 March. The Group trained on P-47s before it was shipped to Wormingford, England and the 9th AF during November of 1943. The 362nd continued their training under Col Morton D. Magoffin, a veteran of almost six years of fighter experience. The Group's assigned squadrons were the 377th, 378th, and 379th.

The Group flew its first mission (a milk-run) on 8 February 1944, escorting B-24s to a V-1 launching site near Pas de Calais. The 362nd continued to fly bomber escort missions until April of 1944 when they switched over to the tactical role. The Group concentrated on attacking German communications in northern France and Belgium as part of the softening up process prior to D-Day. On D-Day the 362nd FG escorted C-47s carrying paratroops to drop zones in Normandy.

The Group continued to fly a variety of missions throughout the Normandy Campaign. Most of which were tactical, but occasionally there would be the opportunity to mix it up with the Luftwaffe. On 20 August 1943 the 362nd shot down six German aircraft while losing two P-47s. 1Lt Joseph Z. Matter accounted for four of the six, claiming four Me 109s. He blew one up at such close range that his canopy was splattered with blood. He destroyed another German aircraft on 8 November 1944 to become an ace — a difficult task for those flying in the tactical role.

The 362nd FG was awarded a DUC for a maximum continuous effort against shipping in the harbor at Brest. Flying through a heavy overcast and intense defensive flak, the Group damaged two cruisers attempting to break out. One was left beached and burning as the Jugs continued to strafe troop ships and bomb shore installations. Merchant ships, motor vessels, and other small naval vessels also received their share of attention.

Col Joseph L. Laughlin replaced Col Magoffin on 10 August 1944. On 20 October 1944 Laughlin led two squadrons carrying 1,000 pound bombs on a dive bombing raid on a small earthen dam near Dieuze. They attacked through a hail of flak and scored ten direct hits on the dam causing a breach that allowed the water to flow out. The action prevented any attempt by the Germans to later blow up the dam and impede the Third Army's advance through the area.

The Group flew tactical and interdiction missions during the Battle of the Bulge during December of 1944 and January of 1945. On 22 January Capt Wilfred B. Crutchfield, leading the 378th FS, spotted a large concentration of approximately 1500 vehicles at Prum. These were units of the German 6th Panzer Army preparing to counterattack. During the action that followed the P-47s destroyed 315 motor vehicles, 11 tanks, six armored cars, and 16 horse drawn wagons.

The Group's second DUC was awarded for actions in the Moselle-Rhine River triangle on 16 March 1945. They surprised the German troops, destroying three tanks, six armored vehicles, 35 rail cars, and over 400 transports. They also destroyed guns and caused numerous troop casualties.

The 362nd FG ceased operations on 1 May 1945 having accounted for 117 enemy aircraft destroyed in combat. Col Magoffin accounted for five of these while flying with the HQ Flight, the 377th FS scored another 34, the 378th claimed 46, and the 379th finished with 32 victories. Capt Edwin G. Fisher of the 377th and 379th FSs was the top scorer with six (five Fw 190s and an Me 109). Lt Joseph E. Matte of the 378th FS had five, and Lt. Kent C. Geyer of the 379th was the high scorer in the 379th with three kills.

The 362nd Group's P-47s remained in their natural metal finish. A red fin and rudder tip were used as Group markings. The aircraft usually carried the black ID bands on the vertical and horizontal tail surfaces as well. The 377th FS had an 18-inch red cowl band, the 378th FS used an 18-inch green cowl band, and the 379th FS employed an 18-inch yellow cowl band. The **377th Squadron's** code letters were **E4**, the 378th used **G8**, and the **379th** had **B8**.

A bombed up *Gooch* rolls out on a pierced steel planking (PSP) taxiway at Airfield A-79 shortly after the Normandy invasion. The P-47D-30-RE was assigned to the 377th FS, 362nd FG. (D. W. Weatherill)

Olive drab Jugs of the 378th FS, 362 FG are serviced at an advanced base in France during the summer of 1944. The jerry cans are emptied into the fuel bowser which was towed to the aircraft on the flightline. A fast turnaround and another sortie were the norm.

Camouflaged P-47s alongside natural metal P-47s were a common sight during mid-1944. These Thunderbolts of the 378th FS, 362nd FG take off from Air Strip A-12 in Normandy during July of 1944.

B8*V, a P-47D-11-RE of the 379th FS, 362nd FG, went through a number of name changes during its career. Lt Floyd Mills named it *The Mighty Mills*, Lt Harold J. Sullivan changed it to *Little Friend*, and it later carried the name *Lil Shinni*. (Author's Collection)

365th Fighter Group

After being authorized on 27 April 1943, the 365th FG was activated on 15 May 1943 and began combat training on P-47s. The Group moved to England on 22 December 1943 and flew its first combat mission from Gosfield on 22 February 1944 when it escorted bombers to Leeuwen, Holland. This mission marked the start of OPERATION ARGUMENT — the systematic destruction of Luftwaffe fighter production. The 365th FG's part, however, was a milk run.

The 365th was commanded by Lt Col Lance Call who had earned his wings as an enlisted man in the US Navy during 1928. He had also served in the US Marine Corps and the Texas National Guard. By 1939 he was flying Short Sunderland flying boats for the RAF. On the Group's first mission the formation was led by Lt Col Oscar H. Coen, an officer on loan from another unit. Lt Col Call led the second flight in order to gain some experience... .

The Group adopted the name 'Hellhawks' and on 5 March 1944 moved to Beaulieu. The 365th stood down on 8 March 1944 to begin training in dive bombing techniques. The first dive bombing mission, led by Maj R. L. Coffey, Jr. was flown to Conches where they made a successful dive bombing attack. Two P-47s were damaged during the attack. 1Lt V. L. Roe was awarded a Distinguished Flying Cross (DFC) when he managed to bring his oil covered Thunderbolt home to an emergency airfield, despite a near complete loss of outward visibility due to the oil covering the windscreen and canopy.

The Group renewed their dive bombing operations prior to D-Day hitting bridges, gun positions, and airfields in an all out attack against German assets that could be used to resist the invasion. The Group also took part in OPERATION CHATTANOOGA CHOO-CHOO on 20 May 1944 — a concerted effort to knock out the German rail transportation network and isolate the battlefields around Normandy. Over the next two weeks the 9th AF damaged 475 locomotives and cut the rail lines at 150 points. The 365th played a major role in this operation. They also took part in OPERATION NO BALL, a series of air strikes aimed at German V 1 launching sites in and around Pas De Calais.

After D-Day the Group moved to Azeville, France on 28 June 1944 where they continued their dive bombing operations during the Battle of Normandy. During early July the 365th FG went after targets near St Lo to aid the Allied breakout. They continued to support the drive across northern France during August and September and later flew patrols in support of the airborne operations in Holland. They were awarded a Belgian Forragere for their part in the liberation of Belgium during this period. During the fall of 1944 they provided direct air to ground support to the troops around Aachen, Germany and the later drive towards the Rhine River.

On 21 October the 365th FG earned its first DUC for putting up 36 aircraft in a fighter sweep over the Bonn-Dusseldorf area. Reaching Euden at 1500 hours the Group was vectored to several formations of German aircraft and immediately engaged them. When the smoke had cleared the Group had accounted for 21 Fw 190s destroyed, 11 damaged, and several probables. Four pilots were awarded the Silver Star and two received DFCs. Six pilots had scored double victories. 2Lt Robert S. Hagan's fighter was hit during the action forcing him to make a crash-landing. His P-47 cartwheeled on landing and sheared off both wings, the engine, and tail section, but the sturdy Republic cockpit held together and Hagan walked away with a minor head injury and some cracked ribs.

A second Belgian award was earned for actions during the Battle of the Bulge. During this period Col Ray Stecker replaced Col Call and while Stecker was CO the Group was awarded its second DUC for its actions on 20 April 1945. Stecker in turn was replaced by Lt Col R. C. Richardson III on 26 April after the Group was transferred to Fritzlar, Germany. The Group welcomed Richardson that day by wiping out a combined German ammunition dump and petrol and benzene storage depot. The attack devastated an area of 18 by 10 square kilometers.

The last combat mission was flown on 8 May 1945. Lt William L. Ward, one of the first pilots to have reported to the Group during May of 1943, was one of the pilots participating in the last mission. Another Hellhawk, Capt Walter W Irvin, remained in the post-war USAF and later set a world speed record of 1404.9 mph while flying an F-104 at Edwards AFB on 16 May 1958.

The 365th FG flew 1241 missions during its tour of duty and lost 46 pilots in action and another 23 in accidents. The Group scored a total of 120.5 aerial victories with an additional 139 enemy aircraft destroyed on the ground. The HQ Flight scored 12 victories, the 386th FS claimed 49, the 387th another 17, and the 388th FS downed 42.5. Maj Robert L. Coffey, Jr. was the top scorer with six victories. Major James E. Hill claimed five.

For most of the war the Group markings were simple — a 12-inch yellow band around the center of the cowl. In some instances an 18-inch black band was also added to the cowl. During early 1945 the squadrons were assigned their own colors, the 385th was given red, the 386th used yellow, and the 388th wore white. Some cowls then began to sport individual designs, blazes, and three color bands. The 365th Fighter Group was assigned the code name 'Frosty'. The **386th FS** was given the code letters **D5** and the code name 'Plastic'. The **387th FS** was coded **B4** with the name 'Blue Bird', while the **388th FS** was coded **C4** and assigned the name 'Elwood'.

Apparently lacking a helmet and headphones, Capt George W. King of the 386th FS, 365th FG, taxis his pristine P-47D-30-RE (D5*C) past a quad fifty caliber anti-aircraft machine gun mount at Chievres, Belgium during the early winter of 1945. (USAAF)

A striped and bombed up *"COFFEY'S POT"* taxis out for a mission on D-Day. The P-47D-25-RE (C4*Y/42-26407) was the mount of Lt Col Robert L. Coffey, the CO of the 388th FS, 365th FG. Coffey served in Congress after the war, but was later killed in the crash of a Lockheed P-80 Shooting Star in New Mexico. (J. V. Crow)

PENGIE II was an olive drab over neutral gray P-47D-10-RE flown by Sqdn/Ldr B. Michael Gladych, a Polish RAF pilot serving with the 61st FS, 56th FG, 8th AF.

Gladych later upgraded to a natural metal P-47D-22-RE which he named *PENGIE III*.

PENGIE V was a midnight blue over sky blue P-47M-1-RE flown by Sqdn/Ldr Gladych towards the end of the war. The 56th FG adopted a number of flamboyant camouflage schemes during the waning months of WW II.

Capt Donovan Smith flew *"OLE COCK III"*, a P-47D-26-RA assigned to the 61st FS, 56th FG, 8th AF. Years later *General* Donovan Smith commanded NATO air forces in Turkey.

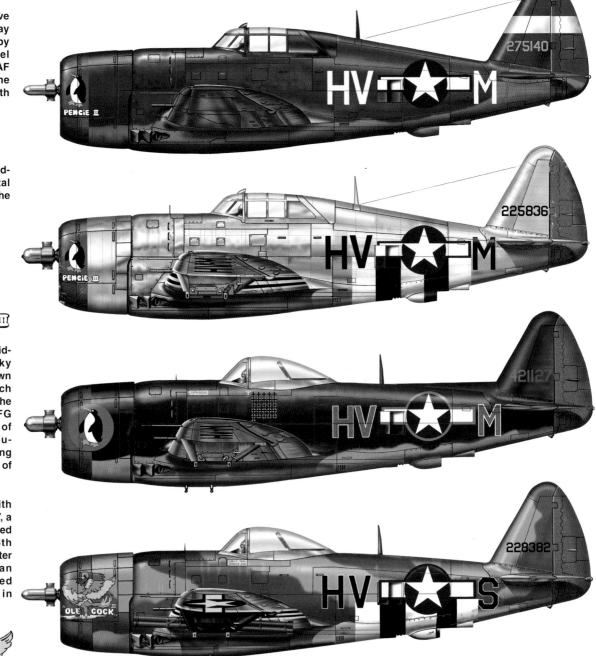

(Below) *The Spirit of Atlantic City, N. J.* was donated by that city and flown by Capt Walker 'Bud' Mahurin of the 63rd FS, 56th FG. The P-47D-5-RE carried the standard olive drab and neutral gray camouflage scheme with white theater recognition bands on the cowl ring. (Author's Collection)

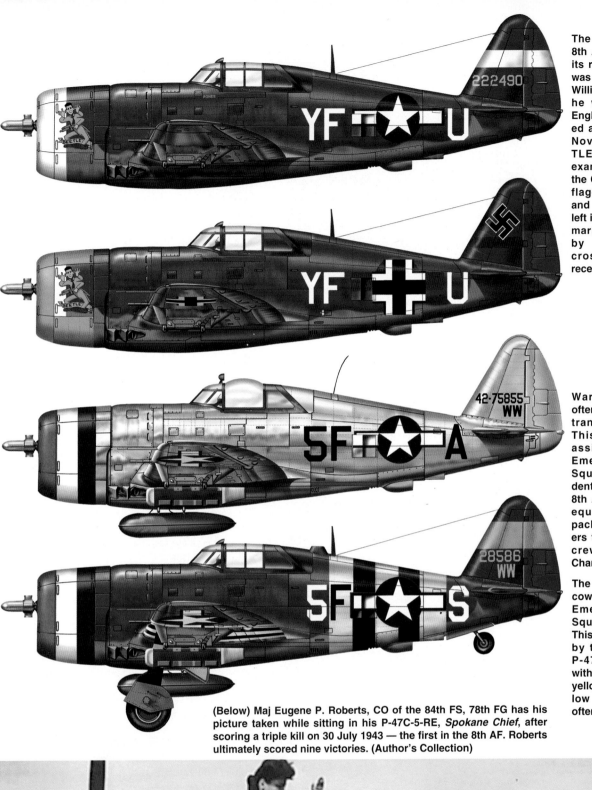

The 358th FS, 355th FG, 8th AF had "BEETLE" on its rolls. The P-47D-2-RA was lost when the pilot, Lt William E. Roach, thinking he was over southern England, mistakenly landed at Caen, France on 7 November 1943. "BEETLE" was thoroughly examined and tested by the Germans. The camouflage scheme, nose art, and fuselage codes were left intact, but the national markings were replaced by oversized German crosses. The Jug also received a yellow cowl.

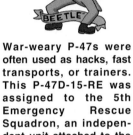

War-weary P-47s were often used as hacks, fast transports, or trainers. This P-47D-15-RE was assigned to the 5th Emergency Rescue Squadron, an independent unit attached to the 8th AF. These Jugs were equipped with dinghy packs and smoke markers to assist downed aircrews in the English Channel.

The red, white, and blue, cowl bands were the 5th Emergency Rescue Squadron unit marking. This war-weary (indicated by the WW on the tail) P-47D-5-RA is marked with invasion stripes and yellow tail bands. The yellow bands were another often used unit marking.

(Below) Maj Eugene P. Roberts, CO of the 84th FS, 78th FG has his picture taken while sitting in his P-47C-5-RE, *Spokane Chief*, after scoring a triple kill on 30 July 1943 — the first in the 8th AF. Roberts ultimately scored nine victories. (Author's Collection)

Engines idling, these olive drab Jugs of the 389th FS, 366th FG prepare for a bomber escort mission to the railroad marshaling yards at Louvain, Belgium on 25 May 1944. The 389th FS was based at Thruxton, England. The lead P-47 was named *Battlin Betty*.

Battlin Betty and her cohorts were joined by the Jugs of the 366th FG's 390th FS for the escort mission to Louvain. Each Thunderbolt carries a 108 gallon fuel tank on the centerline and is wearing oversized US insignia under both wings. (USAAF)

Col Harold N. Holt, CO of the 366th FG led the mission to the Louvain marshaling yards. Most of the 390th FS's fighters are carrying 500 lb bombs in addition to the centerline fuel tank. *Magic Carpet* flew 175 missions without an abort right up to VE-Day — 8 May 1945. (USAAF)

366th Fighter Group

The 366th Fighter Group was activated on 1 June 1943 and moved to Membury, England during December of 1943 and January of 1944. The Group moved to Thruxton on 1 March 1944.

The Group's first mission was a fighter sweep along the French coast on 14 March. They flew their first dive bombing mission the next day, hitting the runways at St Valery airfield in France. The 366th then embarked on a series of pre D-Day softening up missions. On D-Day the Group provided close support, hitting motor convoys and troop and gun positions. During the following days the 366th FG was moved to landing ground A-1 at St Pierre du Mont in France. On 10 July, the Group took off on a mission to dive bomb pillboxes in the St Lo area. The weather was poor and the Group, flying in mist and rain under a 1000 foot cloud base, failed to locate the assigned targets. While still in the area, one of the flight leaders spotted a tank and made a strafing run on it. The tank fired back along with several others in the vicinity. It quickly became clear that the Group had stumbled upon a mass formation of some 50 German tanks preparing for a counterattack on Isigny. The Group leader, Col Harold N. Holt, ordered the Group to attack since they were still carrying their bomb loads. The Jugs battered the panzer force forcing it to retreat and leave approximately 20 wrecked tanks behind. Low on fuel and out of ammunition, the Group returned to base to refuel and rearm. By the time they returned the panzers had regrouped and were advancing about a quarter of a mile from the Allied lines. Another 15 German tanks were destroyed by the Group's Thunderbolts. A third mission flown in a driving rain storm took another panzer column by surprise and it too was routed. These attacks prevented the Germans from breaking through the Allied lines with a large armored force. The 366th FG was awarded a DUC for their actions.

During the remaining months of 1944 the Group continued to provide close tactical support to Allied troops on the continent. The 366th FG also participated in OPERATION MARKET GARDEN, the Allied airborne landings in Holland, by striking flak positions in and around Eindhoven.

On 1 January 1945 the Luftwaffe sent a swarm of approximately 50 Me 109s and Fw 190s against the 366th's Airstrip Y-29 near Asche, Belgium. This was part of the Luftwaffe's mass strike (known as OPERATION BODENPLATTE) on Allied air bases throughout northern Europe. A flight of eight P-47s that had just taken off jettisoned their bombs and tore into the swarm of German aircraft while other 366th Jugs roared off to join the fight. The first flight of eight P-47s shot down 12 Luftwaffe fighters, while the AA gunners claimed another seven. The 352nd Group, which was sharing Y-29, quickly got into the fight and claimed 23 more German fighters. A lone 366th FG pilot had to bail out, but later came peddling back on a borrowed bicycle, none the worse for the wear.

The Group continued its role of providing ground support and on 24 January 1945 destroyed 159 motor transports, 12 tanks, 30 armored vehicles, 4 horse drawn carts, and 47 gun positions. One month later on 22 February, Lt David B. Fox shot down an Arado 234 jet bomber northeast of Aachen — the third 9th AF jet kill of the war. The last mission of the war took place on 3 May 1945 when the Group hit the harbors and shipping at Kiel and Flensburg. The 366th FG remained in the army of occupation after V-E day.

The 366th FG scored a total of 78 victories during its

operations in Europe. The Group HQ Flight claimed 2.5 victories, the 389th Fighter Squadron 23, the 390th FS 35.5, and the 391st FS rounded out the total with 17 kills. The top scorers were Col Dyke F. Meyer, the first Group Commander who claimed two kills with the HQ Flight, 1Lt Edward W. Purdy of the 389th FS who scored three, 1Lt Melvin R. Paisley of the 390th who made ace with five, and Capt Carl J. Johnson of the 391st FS who claimed three.

The 366th FG did not use any official group or squadron color markings, although some natural metal Jugs had every other cowl flap painted black. The fighter's propeller hubs carried a variety of colors and some of these wore spiral or barber pole designs. The Group retained their D-Day invasion stripes until the war's end. The **389th FS** was assigned the fuselage code **A6**, the **390th FS** was given **B2**, and the **398th FS** received **A8**.

367th Fighter Group

The 367th FG was formed on 26 May 1943 and called to active duty on 15 July. The Group and its three squadrons (the 392nd, 393rd, 394th FS) began training on the Bell P-39 before being ordered to Stony Cross, England during March and April of 1944. While at Stony Cross the Group flew P-38s and did not convert to the P-47 until February of 1945. By then the Group was based at St Dizier, France under the command of Col Edwin S. Chickering. The Group had already won a DUC for a mission flown on 25 August 1944.

The Group was awarded a second DUC while flying P-47s on 19 March 1945. Orders were issued for an attack on the headquarters compound of the German Commander-in-Chief, West located at Ziegenburg, Germany. This was the nerve center of operations for the German forces on the western front. The site was built in mountainous terrain and heavily ringed with anti-aircraft guns which rendered any low level air attack extremely difficult. All three squadrons took part in the mission and attacked the target at close intervals. Due to ground haze the Group went in at low level — laying their bombs dead center on the buildings in the compound. The bombing runs were followed up with several strafing runs. When they left the HQ compound was a shambles. The strike caused a critical disruption of the HQ's vital operations and had struck a demoralizing blow to the entire German army on the western front. Despite the heavy air defenses, the Group did not lose a single aircraft.

On 9 April 1945 the 367th FG played a major role in the 9th AF's destruction of enemy aircraft on the ground. They destroyed 60 aircraft and damaged an additional 39 against the loss of a single Thunderbolt to flak. One flight of 14 Jugs destroyed 25 Me 109s and two Me 262 jet fighters while damaging a further 18 Me 109s and an Me 262. The main force of the Group strafed aerodromes at Marienberg and Michelsberg and destroyed 17 aircraft and damaged a further 18. It was this formation that lost the lone Thunderbolt. The 367th FG flew its last mission on 8 May 1945. At the war's end the Group was based at Frankfort/Eschborn in Germany.

Capt Jack Wilk and 1Lt Hoyt W. Benge were the leading scorers for the 392nd FS with 1.5 victories each. 1Lt John L. Dean led the 393rd FS with two kills. No pilot from the 394th FS had a victory with the P-47.

The P-47s flown by the 367th FG were initially transferred from the 354th FG and left in their natural metal finish.

A somewhat irritated Lt Floyd N. Hass of the 398th FS, 366th FG surveys *Peg O' My Heart* after he bellied her in during late 1944. *Peg*, a P-47D-20-RE, had been hit by flak which damaged the port wing and tore off the port flap. (Larry Davis)

Toula, The DUCHESS was a P-47D-27-RE of the 391st FS, 366th FG. The natural metal Jug wears a black cowl ring and recognition bands on the tail and retains her invasion stripes. US insignia are placed under both wings — a common occurrence owing to the Jug's close proximity to the often trigger happy anti-aircraft gunners of the Allied ground forces. (Larry Davis)

H5*B was a P-47D-30-RA of the 392nd FS, 367th FG. The underlined 'B' indicates the presence of another Jug in the squadron with a 'B' code letter. (Weatherill)

3T*H was a P-47D-30-RA assigned to the 22nd FS, 36th FG, 9th AF used in the close support role during the later months of WW II.

Col Joe Laughlin, the Commanding Officer of the 362nd FG, flew FIVE BY FIVE, a P-47D-30-RA, while stationed at Straubing, Germany during May of 1945. The red, blue, and yellow checked cowl combined the colors of the three squadrons assigned to the 362nd FG.

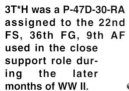

1Lt Don Kark flew this natural metal P-47D22-RA while assigned to the 387th FS, 365th FG, 9th AF.

The 393rd FS, 367th FG, 9th AF flew this P-47D-28-RA in the tactical fighter-bomber role. The blue cowl was a squadron marking, while the vertical stripes on the tail were a group marking.

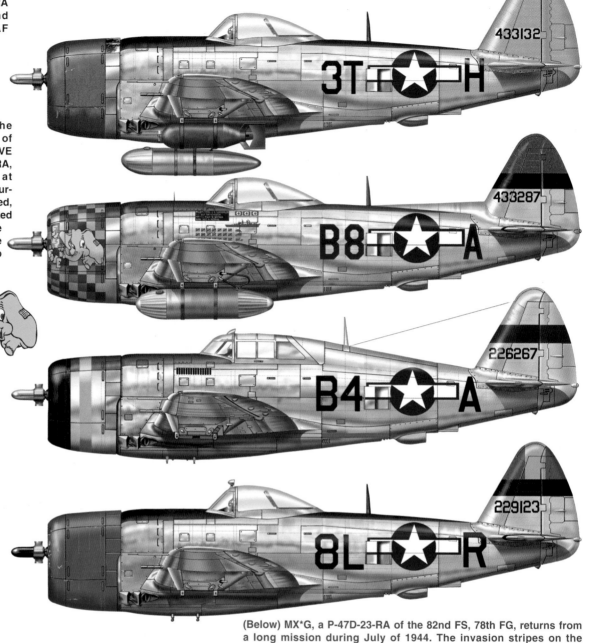

(Below) MX*G, a P-47D-23-RA of the 82nd FS, 78th FG, returns from a long mission during July of 1944. The invasion stripes on the upper fuselage half have been removed, but those on the lower half remain. (Author's Collection)

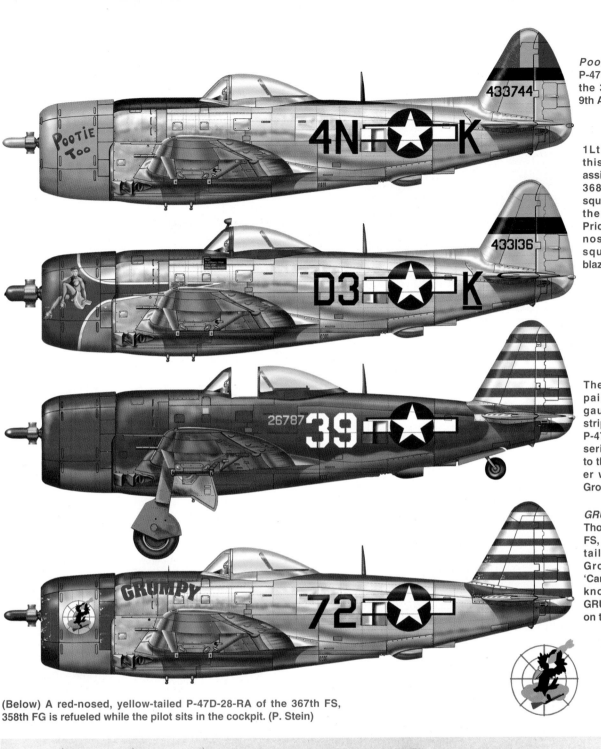

Pootie Too was a P-47D-30-RA assigned to the 394th FS, 367th FG, 9th AF.

1Lt Clifford Price flew this P-47D-30-RE while assigned to the 397th FS, 368th FG, 9th AF. The squadron was known as the 'Jabo Angels'. 1Lt Price superimposed his nose art over the squadron's blue cowl blaze.

The 12th AF's 86th FG painted their tails in gaudy red and white stripes. As a result, this P-47D-27-RE has had its serial number relocated to the fuselage. The fighter was assigned to the Group's 525th FS.

GRUMPY was flown by Lt Thomas Ellis of the 527th FS, 86th FG, 12th AF. The tail stripes earned the Group the nickname 'Candy Stripers'. It is not known if the name GRUMPY was a comment on the pilot's demeanor.

(Below) A red-nosed, yellow-tailed P-47D-28-RA of the 367th FS, 358th FG is refueled while the pilot sits in the cockpit. (P. Stein)

1Lt Donald F. Gelhaus of the 393rd FS, 367th FG flew *Green Devil* (8L*Q). The fin fillet was painted white even though the squadron's color was blue. (D. F. Gelhaus)

Pootie Too was a natural metal P-47D-30-RA flown by Lt Jack T. Curtis of the 394th FS, 367th FG at Airfield Y-74 in Germany. The Squadron painted their cowls overall yellow, while the group marking — red, yellow, and blue vertical bands (front to rear) — were painted on the vertical stabilizer tip above the black ID band. (Weatherill)

PATTI and *Pootie Too*, P-47Ds of the 394 FS, 367th FG, are parked at Airfield Y-74 in Germany. *PATTI* was the mount of Lt George Crokers, while Lt Jack T. Curtis flew *Pootie Too*. Both aircraft are equipped with paddle bladed propellers. (Weatherill)

For a brief time, the fighters continued to be flown in the 354th's markings. Eventually, the Thunderbolts received their own squadron colors and fuselage codes. The colors were red for the 392nd, blue for the 393rd, and yellow for the 394th. The colors were painted over the entire cowl. Some aircraft also had the cowl flaps painted in the squadron colors while others had every other cowl flap painted. The **392nd FS** was assigned the code **HS**, the **393rd** was given **8L**, and the 394th received **4N**. All of the P-47s were assigned a group tail marking which used all three squadron colors in vertical stripes on the tips of the fin and rudder above a black ID band. The tip colors were red, yellow, and blue from front to rear.

368th Fighter Group

Orders authorizing the formation of the 368th Fighter Group were issued on 24 May 1943. The Group was activated on 1 June at Westover Field, Massachusetts under the command of Lt Col Gilbert L. Meyers. The original cadre of personnel departed for Orlando, Florida on 3 June for training and returned to Westover on 6 July. On 23 August the 395th and 396th Squadrons moved to Republic Field, Farmingdale, NY while the 397th was sent to Mitchell Field, NY to train with P-47s. The Group was ordered to England and the 9th AF in late December of 1943. They arrived at their base at Greenham Common, England on 13 January 1944.

The 368th FG's first mission was a fighter sweep to Fecamp, France on 14 March 1944. They flew another sweep the next day to Lille where flak damaged one Thunderbolt. On 24 March, the Group hit Bernay St Martin airfield in their first dive-bombing mission. The mission was without incident, but the next day, the Group ran into the Luftwaffe for the first time. Three German fighters were shot down, five were damaged, while another aircraft was listed as probably destroyed. Two P-47s were damaged during the fight.

On 13 April 1944 the 368th conducted its first attack on a V-1 launch site near Calais. The Group destroyed nine locomotives and damaged four the next day on a strafing mission against German rail stock in France. Their first fighter sweep into Germany took place on 22 April when they visited targets at Duren-Bonn and Koblenz. One P-47, flown by Capt James Goodwin, was lost on the mission.

The Group attacked and destroyed the railroad bridge at Namur on 12 May 1944. This was the first of 33 bridges destroyed and 46 damaged by the Group — a run that would earn the Group the title of 'Bridge Busters' of the 9th AF. On D-Day and D+1 the 368th FG flew 269 sorties destroying or damaging 398 German motor vehicles and were credited, along with two other groups, for saving the troops on Omaha Beach. The 368th FG became the first group to land in Normandy on 13 June and on 19 June the Group moved en masse to Strip Number Three at Cardenville — the first to be stationed on the Continent. While supporting the US 2nd and 3rd Armored Divisions on 25 and 26 July, the Jugs destroyed or damaged 107 tanks and 155 motor transports. The 368th flew cover over advancing armored columns and, in a three day period from 12 through 14 August, destroyed or damaged 88 tanks, 392 trucks, three supply dumps, three fuel dumps, five buildings, 10 gun positions, a German HQ building, three rail junctions, and troop concentrations in six wooded areas. On 16 and 17 August they hit 209 German tanks and trucks trapped in the Falaise Pocket. The 368th FG moved up to Chartres, France on 17 August.

While supporting the 3rd Armored Division on 3 September 1944 the 368th destroyed or damaged 524 enemy vehicles in the vicinity of Mons and Maubeuge, Belgium. The Group was awarded a DUC for it actions. The 368th moved three times over the next 22 days in order to keep pace with the rapidly moving ground forces. Operating out of Chievres, Belgium on 6 October 1944, the Group struck the Luftwaffe Air Depot at Breitscheid and left 22 German aircraft burning on the ground. Another 14 aircraft were damaged and nine listed as probably destroyed.

During the German Ardennes offensive on 17 December 1944 the 368th FG shot down 11 German aircraft while the 397th FS was busy destroying 119 tanks and motor transports on one mission, an action that prevented the German capture of St Vith and its beleaguered US garrison. The following day nine more enemy fighters were shot down while the 396th FS, using 500 lb bombs, destroyed 30 German tanks at Stavelot. The 396th also shot up 20 trucks. Three P-47s were hit by flak, but were able to return to base. Seven additional flights of P-47s were sent against these targets and were able to destroy a further 32 armored vehicles and 60 trucks. These strikes were flown at low level through fog bound hills and valleys.

On 27 December the 368th moved to Juvincourt which was followed by a move to Metz, France on 5 January 1945 as the Allies shifted units to deal with the German's Ardennes offensive. Six pilots were lost on 14 January when 12 Thunderbolts were jumped by 50 German fighters. On 22 January 1945 the Group achieved a measure of revenge when they caught — and clobbered — 597 German vehicles retreating from the Ardennes debacle. A follow-up strike the next day added to the scrap heap.

Lt Robert D. Andrus of the 395th FS, 368th FG, flew *LITTLE AUDREY* while based at Nurmberg/Buchschwabach, Germany shortly after the end of the war. *AUDREY* was a P-47D-28-RA.

The Group's bridge-busting efforts continued into the new year when the Bullay bridge was collapsed on 10 February 1945. Medium and heavy bombers had been trying to knock it out for months. The Group continued to harry the retreating Wehrmacht; and in a three day period from 23 to 25 February, the 368th damaged or destroyed 173 tanks, 659 trucks, six locomotives, and 148 freight cars.

The 368th flew its 1,000th mission on 2 March 1945 and celebrated their first full year of combat operations on 14 March by shooting down 10 German aircraft. A record number of 184 sorties were flown on 24 March. As the end of the war neared the Group moved again on 15 April to Frankfurt-Rhein Main Airfield in Germany. The next day they destroyed 57 German aircraft on the ground and followed up on 17 April with a record score of 91 locomotives destroyed or damaged. The last operational mission was flown on 7 May 1945 when the Group flew a fighter sweep into Czechoslovakia. The 368th FG remained in Germany with the occupation forces after the war.

During the period 14 March 1944 through 9 May 1945 the 368th FG flew 1406 missions consisting of 17,455 sorties and totaling 45,390 combat hours. The Group expended 4,570,892 rounds of fifty caliber ammunition and dropped 10,860,000 pounds of bombs. Sixty-nine P-47s were lost in combat and another 31 were damaged beyond repair and written off. Twenty-eight of these were lost to German fighters while a further 47 were claimed by German anti-aircraft fire. The remainder were lost to other causes. Twenty-four pilots were killed in action, 38 were listed as missing in action, and another 11 were wounded. Ten pilots were able to return to US military control after being shot down. Fourteen pilots were injured in accidents.

A pair of 368th FG Jugs fly over a devastated German city. Both P-47s have been repaired using olive drab wing and tail parts from other aircraft. Absorbing battle damage was a way of life for aircraft involved in low-level close support work. (Paul Quilty)

During the same period, the Group claimed 120 enemy aircraft destroyed in the air, 59 damaged, and 20 probably destroyed. The 395th FS claimed 35, the 396th shot down 40, the 397th FS accounted for 44, and HQ Flight had one. The leading scorers were Capt T. N. Montag, Lt W. J. Garry, and Lt Col P. P. Douglas of the 395th with three kills each. Lt Col Douglas also scored 4 victories with the 396th FS making him an ace with 7 kills and the top scorer in the 396th FS. The 397th FS's Maj R. W. Hendrickson also aced out with five, while Lt W. Kerr and Maj Hendricks each had four victories on a single mission.

A further 98 aircraft were destroyed on the ground, 125 damaged, and 15 probably destroyed. Tactical missions accounted for 1101 armored vehicles, 10,801 trucks, 913 locomotives, 7477 freight cars, 79 bridges, 1040 factories or buildings, 246 gun positions, 96 supply dumps, and 146 vessels destroyed or damaged. The Group also accomplished 475 rail cuts, and attacked 260 railroad yards and 50 airfields.

The Group's aircraft were left in the natural metal finish common among USAAF units late in the war. The Group marking consisted of a yellow fin and rudder tip painted above the black recognition band. Each of the fighter squadrons were given a color and a fuselage code — the **395th FS** was assigned the color red and the code **A7**, the **396th** was given yellow and **8L**, and the **397th FS** used blue and **D3**. There is some evidence that the **396th FS** also used the code **C2** at one time. The 395th FS used the nickname Panzer Dusters, the 396th Thunder Bums, and the 397th FS Jabo Angels.

LEAKY JOE was a razorbacked P-47D flown by Capt Irving Ostuw of the 396th FS, 368th FG. The cowl flaps have been decorated with playing card symbols. Ostuw scored two kills on 7 April 1945. (Paul Quilty)

Margo was a P-47D-28-RA assigned to the 405th FS, 511th FS.Natural metal P-47s usually wore black ID bands on their tail — in this case, rather hastily applied as evidenced by the overspray on the fin. The yellow canopy frame was a squadron marking.

"*I'LL GET BY*" was a P-47D-27-RE assigned to the 506th FS, 404th FG, 9th AF. The aircraft wears three black and two white invasion stripes versus the standard three white and two black strips. A black and white leaf design was also painted on the leading edge of the bomb racks. "*I'LL GET BY*" is fully loaded with three 500 lb bombs and four five-inch HVARs.

Rear fuselage and tail of "*I'LL GET BY*".

(Below) A pair of P-47Ds of the 497th FS, 368th FG flies high over the Bavarian Alps during early 1945. The 497th was known as the 'Jabo Angels' and had a blue blaze on the cowl and fuselage as a squadron marking. The yellow fin tip was a Group marking.

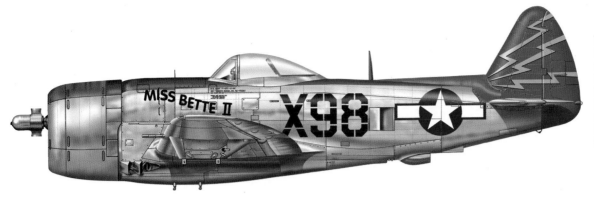

The 79th FG's P-47s had a striking group marking of yellow lightning bolts on a blue fin and rudder. *MISS BETTE II*, was assigned to the Group's 87th Fighter Squadron.

P-47s assigned to the 324th FG had their fuselage emblazoned with lightning bolts painted in the squadron color. *Amy Lou* was a P-47D-27-RE assigned to the Group's 314th FS.

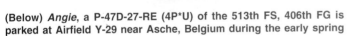

The 'Checkertail Clan' traded in their P-40s for P-47s during the fall of 1943. *CHERRY MARY/SPIRIT OF DeSOTO COUNTY* was flown by Lt Lamarr Perry of the 318th FS, 325th FG, 15th AF while stationed at Foggia, Italy during the spring of 1944.

(Below) *Angie*, a P-47D-27-RE (4P*U) of the 513th FS, 406th FG is parked at Airfield Y-29 near Asche, Belgium during the early spring of 1945. (John J. Quincy via Stanley Wyglendowski)

371st Fighter Group

Formation of the 371st Fighter Group was authorized on 25 May 1943 with its activation on P-47s following on 15 June at Richmond Army Air Base, Virginia. The Group went overseas with three fighter squadrons — the 404th, 405th, and 406th — during February and March of 1944 and was based at an advanced landing ground at Bisterne, England under the command of Col Bingham T. Kleine.

The Group's first mission was a fighter sweep over the French coast on 12 April 1944. On 20 May the 9th AF initiated OPERATION CHATTANOOGA CHOO-CHOO, an extensive air campaign aimed at the rail transportation network in France. The goal was to paralyze the German rail network and isolate the beaches in and around the Normandy Peninsula. Five hundred fighter-bombers were sent to work over the railroads to keep supplies and reinforcements from moving into the invasion area. In a maximum effort the 371st FG put up 50 Thunderbolts which helped make the day a success as the 9th Air Force destroyed 46 locomotives, probably destroyed 11 more, and damaged an additional 21. Thirty trains were attacked and damaged during these missions. One pilot of the 371st FG was wounded by flak. Another made it back, "nursing and cursing" his blackened Jug which had had two engine cylinders knocked out by a 20mm shell causing it to throw oil all over his P-47.

The 371st FG continued to fly a variety of escort, dive bombing, and fighter sweeps prior to D-Day. The Group patrolled the beaches on D-Day and then conducted an extensive series of close support missions during the Normandy Campaign.

On 8 June the 371st FG drew their first blood against the Luftwaffe when Maj Rockford V. Gray and his wingman ran into seven Fw 190s attacking ships in the Channel off Le Havre. Despite the uneven odds the two pilots engaged the Focke Wulfs. Gray shot down two and caused a third, who was on Gray's tail, to lose control and crash (Gray later became an ace, but was killed in a crash the following September). More 371st Jugs entered the battle and Capt George D. Pieck of the 404th FS and Capt Uno A. Salmi of the 406th each bagged an Fw 190. The 371st FG lost two aircraft, but one wounded pilot bailed out over the Channel and was rescued.

The 371st FG moved to Beuzeville, France during June and played a large part in the Allied breakout at St. Lo on 25 July. The Group moved three more times through the month of December, all to follow the ground forces and provide close support. After taking part in the Battle of the Bulge, the Group moved again — settling in the French fortress city of Metz on 15 February 1945. On 28 February the 371st claimed four aircraft destroyed, two probables, and three damaged while strafing Me 109s and Fw 190s on the ground.

The Group was awarded a DUC for a six day action that contributed to the defeat of the Wehrmacht in southern Germany. The Group flew 1035 sorties and destroyed 18 tanks, 1237 motor vehicles, 158 buildings, 16 gun emplacements, and 366 horse drawn carts. Damage was inflicted on 47 tanks, 1061 motor transports, 80 buildings, 280 horse drawn carts, and 14 gun emplacements. The growing number of horse-drawn carts was perhaps an indicator that the German Army was becoming critically short of fuel and was nearing collapse. During this period the 371st FG lost three Jugs and had to write off a fourth. In addition to the DUC the Group was cited in a Belgian Order of the Day for its efforts from 6 June to 30 September 1944.

Lt James A. Zweizig of the 404th FS joined the ranks of pilots with jet kills when he engaged and destroyed an Me-262 fighter near Eger, Austria on 17 April 1945. The Group flew its last mission on 8 May 1945.

The Group received credit for 62.5 victories while producing a single ace in Major Rockford V. Gray with 6.5 kills (only three of these victories were scored with the 371st FG). The HQ Flight was credited with three victories, the 404th and 405th FSs with 14 kills each, and the 406th with 31.5 victories. The leading squadron scorers were 1Lt Estell L. Stobaugh and 2Lt William R. Myers of the 404th with two each, Maj John W. Leonard of the 405th with 1.5, and Lt Col Sanders E. Delaney of the 406th FS with three victories.

The 371st does not appear to have a unique Group marking until February of 1945 when blue and white cowl flaps were adopted. Each of the squadrons was also assigned a color — red for the 404th FS, blue for the 405th FS, and yellow for the 406th FS. These colors were usually painted on the cowl rings. When the Group was temporarily assigned to the 1st Tactical Air Force during early November of 1944, the vertical fins and rudders were painted red. The black ID bands remained. The red tails were retained after the Group went back to the 9th AF during February of 1945. During this time, the squadron colors were applied to the entire cowling back to the blue and white cowl flaps. The rudders were painted blue — the fins remained red — and the black ID bands on the tail were painted white to help them stand out against the red and blue background. The **404th FS** received the code letters **9Q**, the **405th** was assigned **8N**, and the **406th** was given **4W**. The squadrons were also assigned the call signs 'Kismet', 'Discharge', and 'Yearling' respectively. The Group used the call sign 'Van Dyke'.

9Q*R, a natural metal P-47D-27-RE of the 404th FS, 371st FG moves along a PSP taxiway somewhere on the continent during the summer or fall of 1944. The 404th used a red cowl ring as a squadron marking.

8N*X was a P-47D-28-RA assigned to the 405th FS, 371st FG. The Group was transferred from the 9th AF control to the 1st Tactical Air Force (Provisional) during November of 1944 and adopted blue cowls and fins as a unit marking. The rudder was red. A white ID band runs across the fin, but the serial number is natural metal.

373rd Fighter Group

The 373rd Fighter Group consisted of the 410th, 411th, and 412th Fighter Squadrons and began training after it was activated on 15 August 1943. During March and April of 1944 the Group became part of the 9th AF and was based at Woodchurch, England under the command of Col William H. Schwartz. Their first mission, a fighter sweep over Normandy, took place on 8 May 1944 — one year before the end of the war in Europe. During the pre-invasion period the Group escorted B-26s attacking railroads, airfields, and bridges in France. Once the invasion was launched on 6 June 1944, the Group found itself patrolling the skies over the beaches. During the remaining days of June, they went after roads, troops, tanks, and fuel and ammo dumps.

The 373rd FG moved to Touren-Bassin, France on 19 July 1944 and thereafter continued to attack rail lines, trains, hangars, and warehouses to prevent enemy reinforcements and supplies from reaching St Lo where the Allies had broken through on 25 July . The Group struck troop, armor, and gun positions in the Falaise-Argentan area during August. The 373rd had a field day on 15 August when the 411th FS claimed eight victories and the 412th FS bagged four more. Maj Harry L. Downing of the 411th FS and 1Lt Clarence L. Hough each claimed a pair of German aircraft during the fight. The Group moved to St. James, France on 19 August.

The 373rd FG was sent out to sink barges on the Rhine River on 15 September 1944. One barge was destroyed and six were driven onto the shore. On 29 September the Group claimed 15 barges and a tug boat. The Group moved to Le Culot, Belgium on 22 October 1944 where fortune found them in a position to support US counterattacks during the Battle of the Bulge the following December. The Group concentrated their efforts on highways, bridges, railroads, and marshaling yards. Continuing their attacks on the rail network, the Group destroyed eight locomotives, 346 rail cars, and 40 buildings on 22 January 1945.

On 23 February the Jugs found a train that had attempted to hide by pulling into a tunnel near Ehrany. The train was too long for the tunnel leaving 25 exposed cars at the south end and another five exposed at the north end. The P-47s destroyed everything in sight and left the middle of the train stuck in the tunnel.

Another base change — to Venlo, Holland — took place on 11 March 1945. This move set up one of the Group's most successful missions and earned them a DUC in the process. With the crossing of the Rhine River imminent, the Group flew six missions on 20 March attacking enemy airfields and communication lines. They destroyed 119 enemy aircraft and rendered three airfields inoperable. Next, the Group flew through German flak barrages to knock out rail lines, rolling stock, motor vehicles, and disrupt the main highways — all without losing a single P-47. Their last large-scale mission took place on 11 April when

they encountered over 20 Fw 190s while strafing an airfield. The Group claimed 17 destroyed, four probables, and two damaged. The Group's last mission, a 'show-of-force' flight over the Klote area, was flown on 6 May 1945.

In addition to its DUC the 373rd FG was awarded the French Croix de Guerre during August of 1944, was cited in the Belgian Order of the Day on 10 October 1944, and was awarded the Belgian Fourragere.

The 373rd FG scored 110 victories with the HQ Flight claiming 3.5, the 310th FS scoring 23, the 311th destroying 45.5, and the 312th rounding out the total with 38. The top scoring ace was 1Lt Edward B. Edwards, Jr. of the 411th FS with 5.5. 1Lt Davis L. King of the 412th FS had five, but one of these was claimed while he was flying with the 363rd FG. 1Lt Talmadge E. Ambrose of the 410th FS scored all four of his kills on 8 April 1945.

The 373rd FG did not use any distinguishing group or squadron markings, however, the Group's aircraft did wear the standard black recognition bands on the tail surfaces of its natural metal P-47s. The **410th FS** was assigned the code **R3**, the **411th U9**, and the **412th FS V5**.

Windy City, a P-47D-28-RA, was named by pilot Lt W. J. Garrett in honor of Chicago. Garrett, assigned to the 410th FS, 373rd FG, was stationed at the snow-covered field at Le Coulet, Belgium. (J. V. Crow)

Lt Staryl C. Austin, Jr's P-47D-30-RA undergoes its 100-hour check at Venlo, Holland during April of 1945. Austin was assigned to the 410th FS, 373rd FG. (J. V. Crow)

A tight formation of 411th FS P-47Ds cruises enroute to strafe a German build-up. The Jugs are carrying drop tanks under the wings. (W. N. Hess)

French P-47s emulated the camouflage schemes of their US counterparts. This P-47D-28-RE was assigned to GC III/4 of the Free French Air Force. The tail is marked with the Cross of Lorraine and the pre-war style rudder stripes. The Jug also carries the narrow style invasions stripes used on many French P-47s.

C9•U was a natural metal P-47D-30-RA assigned to GC I/4 'Navarre' of the Free French Air Force during 1945. The Thunderbolt has the smaller fin flash painted on the rudder.

The USSR received just under 200 P-47s. *SOVEREIGN SENATORS K. OF P.* was one of the few that arrived via the Alaska-Siberia route. The long distance flights mandated the addition of a direction finding loop on the fuselage spine.

The Brazilian Air Force's 1 Grupo de Caca was assigned to the USAAF's 350th FG for operations over Italy during 1944. This P-47D-25-RE was flown by Lt Alberto Martins Torres. The cowl number denotes 'A Flight', Aircraft Number 4.

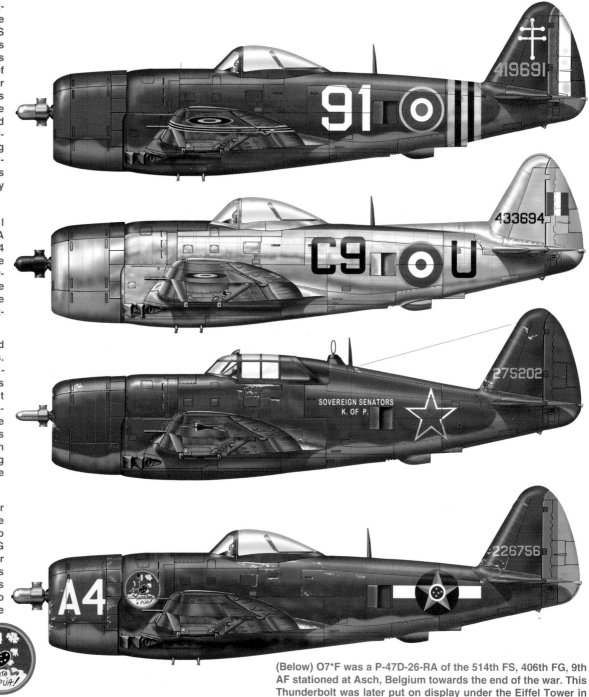

(Below) O7*F was a P-47D-26-RA of the 514th FS, 406th FG, 9th AF stationed at Asch, Belgium towards the end of the war. This Thunderbolt was later put on display under the Eiffel Tower in Paris. (John J. Quincy via Stanley Wyglendowski)

404th Fighter Group

The 404th FG was formed as a dive bomber group on 25 January 1943 and activated on 4 February 1943. While training with P-39s and P-47s during August of 1943, the Group was redesignated the 404th Fighter-Bomber Group. The Group and its three subordinate squadrons — the 506th, 507th, and 508th (all now equipped with Thunderbolts) — moved to Winkton, England during March and April of 1944 under he command of Col Carroll W. McColpin. McColpin was a 29 year old ace who had been a member of one of the RAF Eagle Squadrons.

The 404th FG became operational on 1 May 1944 and suffered its first loss on 9 May when a pilot of the 506th FS was hit by flak and shot down over the rail yard at Serqueux, France. On 19 May 1Lt Benjamin F. Kitchen of the 508th's 'Red Flight' scored the Group's first aerial victory when his flight was jumped by six Me 109s. He turned into the attackers and blew one of them up. Kitchen flew through the debris covering his windscreen with German oil.

Although Winkton was considered an advanced landing ground (and hence lacked a number of the facilities associated with more permanent airfields) the Group remained there to support the Normandy invasion until July of 1944. They provided top cover over the landing beaches on 6 and 7 June and, on 10 June, all three squadrons fanned out over the French countryside on train and bridge-busting missions designed to further isolate the battlefield. The 508th made 14 rail line cuts near Chartres, burned 15 tank cars, blew up a locomotive and switch house, and then strafed a row of barracks. The 507th FS caught a pair of trains approaching a point from opposite directions, cut the tracks in front and behind them, and forced the two trains to halt next to each other. The squadron then proceeded to work both trains over using bombs and machine guns. Bombs blew two cars from one train onto the other. The 506th FS blasted a highway bridge, tore up a rail intersection and destroyed an engine and 15 freight cars.

On 6 July 1944 the 404th FG packed up and took their show on the road, moving to Chapelle, France. During July the Group attacked gun positions and enemy transports in the St Lo area and received a French Croix de Guerre with Palm for assisting the 1st Army at St. Lo. A tragic event later took place on 24 July when an Allied bomber accidentally dropped its load on the base,

Mary Ann gets her tail washed by a ground crewman. This P-47D-30-RA was assigned to the 506th FS of the 404th FG. (Jeff Ethell)

More 404th FG aircraft sit on an abandoned German airfield which is in surprisingly good condition. Included is a venerable razorbacked P-47D-22-RE of the 507th Fighter Squadron. The advancing tactical fighter units tended to occupy German airfields as fast as the Luftwaffe abandoned them. (USAF)

killing four of the Group's members, wounding another 14, and destroying two P-47s.

While supporting the 3rd Armored Division on 15 August the 404th FG flew 11 missions to bomb the town of Ranes twice and strafe the surrounding area a number of times. At the days end the score stood at 29 German tanks, five half-tracks, 12 other armored vehicles, 35 trucks, and five gun positions destroyed.

The Group earned a DUC on 10 September for close support in the Amien-Julich-Duren area. The weather was miserable and the defensive flak was intense, but the 404th ignored both and destroyed 24 locomotives and 100 freight cars, damaged another 200 cars, cut 32 rail lines, knocked out two bridges and strafed and bombed factories and communication facilities. The Group moved to St Trond, Belgium during the fall of 1944 and received the Belgian Forragere for its contribution to the liberation of Belgium.

During the battle of the Bulge on 17 December the 404th tangled with the Luftwaffe claiming 12 enemy aircraft destroyed and six damaged, while losing two of their own.

During this time Col McColpin had been replaced by Lt Col Leo Moon as the Group Commander. Moon was responsible for two armament improvements. He consulted the Republic Technical Representative about what could be done to prevent gun barrel burn outs. The Tech Rep advised him to remove the blast tubes around the barrels to provide better cooling during missions, but have them replaced *after* the mission to protect the guns from dew and rust. Moon followed the advice and never had another gun barrel burn out. He also had an additional set of switches attached to the two outboard guns on each side. By firing only four guns at a time, Moon saved ammunition for additional targets. All of the guns were boresighted at 300 yards which retained a lethal cone of fire. When the inboard guns ran out of ammunition he could simply flip a switch and keep on firing. On 22 February Lt Col Moon led the Group on four missions as part of OPERATION CLARION. By the end of the day the results added up to 25 locomotives, 124 rail cars, 3 factories, and 12 other buildings destroyed. Twenty-four tracks were cut and six locomotives and 68 rail cars were damaged. The Group's last mission was flown on 4 May 1945.

The Group ended the war with 47 enemy aircraft downed in aerial combat. The 506th FS had 16 kills, the 507th claimed 17, and the 508th FS scored 13. One kill was credited to the Group HQ Flight. Capt George A. McLaughlin of the 507th FS was the only ace with 7 victories (Col McColpin was also an ace, but most of his victories had been scored with the Eagle Squadron).

The 404th FG did not carry any group or squadron markings beyond the black identification bands on the tail surfaces. The **506th FS** was coded **4K**, the **507th Y8**, and the **508th 7J**.

SWEET MUSIC, a P-47D-30-RA of the 508th FS, 404th FG carries the Group's unofficial marking on the cowl superimposed over a black band. (Larry Davis)

405th Fighter Group

The 405th FG was originally formed as the 405th Bombardment Group (Dive) on 4 February 1943. The Group went on active duty on 1 March 1943 and began training on A-24s, A-25s, P-39s, and P-47s. The Group moved overseas to Christchurch, England during February and March of 1944 and was redesignated the 405th Fighter Bomber Group. The Group consisted of the 509th, 510th, and 511th Fighter Bomber Squadrons.

The first mission, flown on 11 April 1944, was uneventful. The Group then settled into the standard 9th AF fighter-bomber role and worked over German airfields, marshaling yards, and bridges in France prior to D-Day. The 405th patrolled the skies over Brest during the invasion and continued flying armed reconnaissance sorties in support of the Normandy Campaign before moving to Picauville, France on 30 June 1944. On 26 July a patrol found bumper to bumper traffic moving south on a road near Gavray. The fighters strafed both ends of the column forcing it to a halt and then called in additional P-47s. The Group flew over 100 sorties in five hours of near continuous strafing. Over 400 tanks

Lt Billy Doyle flew *HONEY-BUCKET JOE!* while assigned to the 509th FS, 405th FG. The Jug, coded G9*Q, carried rather unusual nose art — part clown and part monster. Billy Doyle was later killed in action. (M. Titre via N. Graser)

(Above) *CHIEF SKI-U-MAH* was a P-47D-27-RE assigned to the 509th FS, 405th FG. The *CHIEF* is taxiing out for a mission loaded with a pair of 500 lb bombs under the wings and a 250 lb bomb under the fuselage. The large area of the P-47s cowling and fuselage side allowed the artwork to be as large as that normally seen on bombers.

(Below) P-47D-28-RA (G9*B/42-28445) *CHOW HOUND 2ND* was the mount of the 509th FS Commander, Capt Blackburn. The 509th was part of the 405th Fighter Group. (Titre via Graser)

43

and motor vehicles were destroyed along with large numbers of German troops.

On 13 August the 405th destroyed 11 locomotives and approximately 130 freight cars in the Argentan area. The next day the Group was flying cover over the US 7th Armored Division near Dreux-Nogent Le Rotro. The 405th FG pilots strafed some trucks until one pilot noticed the Germans were waving white flags. The pilots buzzed the surrendering Germans to get them marching towards the 7th Armored Division and radioed the Division to send men to escort the POWs to a camp.

On 19 August the 405th FG went after light shipping on the Seine River near Melun and sank 13 barges and damaged another 27. On 25 August the Group hit rail traffic in the Soissons-Laon-Reims area, claiming 19 engines and over 170 freight cars. Six more engines were destroyed and a train loaded with Junkers Ju 88 fuselages was shot up at the Neufchateau marshaling yards on 28 August.

On 14 September the Group moved to St Dizier to stay close to the advancing Allied armies. On 24 September the 405th earned a DUC for

FAT CAT, a P-47D-15-RE (2Z*N/42-76216) was assigned to the 510th FS, 405th FG. during the summer of 1944. A pair of eyes adorned the upper cowl ring. The canopy frame is believed to be blue, the 510th's squadron color. Oversized US national insignia were painted under both wings for quick identification. (Author's Collection)

its actions in support of the 4th Armored Division near Chateau Salins. Despite rain and overcast down to 1500 feet the Group found the site of an ongoing tank battle. The pilots went in at 800 feet in the face of intense defensive fire and destroyed a number of enemy tanks. A second squadron, unable to find the tanks, located over 100 German vehicles rushing to reinforce the battle area. After a series of strafing and bombing runs, the remaining vehicles were forced to scatter and turn back.

Margo sits on the airfield at St Dizier, France during September of 1944. The P-47D-28-RA was part of the 511th FS, 405th FG. It is believed that the canopy frame is painted yellow — the 511th's squadron color. Black overspray can be seen just above the black ID band on the vertical fin. (J. V. Crow)

Lt Gabriel Greenwood of the 511th FS, 405th FG gives his new base at Picauville, France a look after arriving on 29 June 1944. Greenwood named his P-47D-20-RE *Knobby* (painted in yellow on the cowl). The white letter 'B' on the rudder trim tab denotes the Squadron's B Flight. (J. V. Crow)

The Group then attacked a German strongpoint, bombing and strafing it until it was completely neutralized. The 405th was also cited by the Belgian government for its part in the liberation of Belgium.

On 25 February 1945, 405th FG pilots encountered an Me 262 jet fighter and damaged it. On 30 March the Group dropped 145 bombs and destroyed 30 aircraft on the ground at Gutersloh Aerodrome. The Group's last big score came on 16 April when they destroyed 67 aircraft

K4*S was a P-47D-22-RE flown by Lt Walter A. Grabowski of the 511th FS, 405th FG. The cowl ring, alternating cowl flaps, and canopy frame are painted yellow. The ID band on the vertical fin and rudder has been painted over with fresh olive drab. (Grabowski via Weatherill)

and damaged another 40 at the Altengrabow Aerodrome. The Group's last mission was flown on 8 May 1945. One A P-47 buzzing a POW Camp flew too low and hit Lake Traun causing it to belly in — the last loss of the war.

The 405th FG was credited with 58 aerial victories. The 509th FS had 15, the 510th FS claimed 30, and the 511th FS scored 13. 2Lt William A. Barrow led the 509th FS with two kills, 1Lt Francis M. Norr led the 510th FS with four, and 1Lt Bill F. Myers was tops in the 511th FS with three kills.

Most of the 405th FG aircraft were left in their natural metal finish and carried no Group markings. During late 1944 squadron colors were added to the leading 18-inches of the cowl — red for the 509th, blue for the 510th, and yellow for the 511th. The **509th squadron** was coded **G9**, the **510th 2Z**, and the **511th K4**. Late in the war some aircraft carried the squadron colors on the tail bands and canopy frames. The 509th and 511th FSs also painted the flight letter in black on the rudder trim tabs. It is believed that the 510th FS also engaged in this practice.

406th Fighter Group

Like the 405th FG, the 406th FG was originally formed as a Dive Bomber Group and activated on 1 March 1943. It was redesignated the 406th Fighter-Bomber Group during August of 1943. The Group moved to Ashford, England during April of 1944 as part of the tactical airpower build-up during the months prior to D-Day. The Group's three squadrons, the 512th, 513th, and 514th Fighter Squadrons, became operational on 9 May 1944 in time to take part in the pre D-Day softening up process.

The 406th provided area cover during the D-Day landings and shifted to close support operations as the Allies advanced during the Normandy Campaign. The Thunderbolts used rockets to destroy two tanks and two four-gun batteries west of Vire on 2 August. On 5 August the 406th FG moved to Tour-en-Bassin, France. The next day the Group was back in action when it hit a German train loaded with 60 tanks and destroyed one fuel train and damaged another.

On 19 August a dozen German fighters caught the 406th FG on its way home after a strafing mission. The Jugs were without ammunition, so they hit the deck at high speed. Their evasive maneuvers caused two of their attackers to fly into the ground, however one P-47 was shot down during the melee.

The 406th FG earned its first DUC on 12 September when it was sent out during the afternoon to locate a column of German vehicles retreating through the Belfort Gap near Chateau Auroux. Thirty-six P-47s caught the column south of the Loire River and, using rockets, bombs, and machine gun fire, destroyed at least 300 vehicles. Low on fuel they went back to base, refueled, rearmed, and returned to wipe out another 187 vehicles. On 29 September the Group engaged a formation of approximately 30 German fighters and shot down six. Three other German fighters were claimed as probables against the loss of two P-47s.

The 406th FG was awarded a second DUC for its actions in the Bastogne area during the Battle of the Bulge. The Group flew 81 missions totaling 529 sorties from dawn until dusk and destroyed 13 enemy aircraft, 610 motor vehicles, 190 tanks, 226 gun positions, 59 buildings, 43 horse drawn wagons, 12 bridges, and 13 ammo or fuel dumps. Three times they arrived just in time to disrupt an all out German assault.

On 26 January 1945 the 406th FG claimed another 119 motor transports and 20 horse carts destroyed at Prum while damaging another 111 vehicles. The Group was involved in three separate aerial engagements on 22 February in which they destroyed a total of 11 enemy aircraft and damaged 8 more. Four Thunderbolts were lost. On 1 March the Group's 512th FS shot down five enemy aircraft and damaged four others. On 22 March the 514th FS struck an aerodrome near Munster and destroyed three Me 410s, 17 Me 109s, and damaged an additional 14 aircraft on the ground without loss. One of their last missions was a leaflet drop on 27 April 1945. The 406th was based at Nordholz, Germany as part of the Army of Occupation until 20 August 1946.

The 406th FG racked up 62 victories during its single year of combat operations over the continent. The 512th FS had 34, the 513th scored 13, and the 514 had 15. 1Lt Doral G. Whicker led the 512th FS with four kills while 1Lts Eldon L. Dunkleberger and Elton V. Kern of the 513th had three each. Capt George I. Ruddell was the high scorer in the 514th FS with three.

The 406th FG's Thunderbolts were left in their natural metal finish. There were no specific Group markings until late in the war when 12-inch horizontal bands of blue, red and yellow were painted on the vertical fin and rudder tip. Each of the three squadrons was also assigned a color — yellow for the 512th FS, red for the 513th, and blue for the 514th FS. These were initially an 18-inch band on the cowl, but late in 1944 took the form a sweeping blaze from the bottom of the cowl to the windscreen. The **512th FS** fighters were coded **L3**, the **513th** was coded **4P**, and the **514th** wore **07**.

A 512th FS P-47D-30-RA displays the Squadron's yellow blaze and the 406th FG's tail marking of horizontal blue, red, and yellow bands. (R. C. Jones via Larry Davis)

(Above) *BIG ASS BIRD II* was a P-47D-30-RA assigned to the 513th FS, 406th FG. 513th Squadron P-47s had a red blaze over the cowling and front fuselage.

(Below) Maj Howard Park (left) flew *BIG ASS BIRD II*. The 413th FS's Jugs were equipped to fire 5-inch High Velocity Aerial Rockets (HVARs) and Maj Park was the first to use the rockets to destroy a German Pzkfw V Panther tank. (Bill Peters)

(Above) *Saucy Susie* has been loaded with two 500 lb bombs and a centerline 250 lb bomb prior to a mission against German ground forces. *Susie* was flown by Lt A. A. Hitch of the 513th FS, 406th FG while stationed at Asche, Belgium during March of 1945. (A. A. Hitch)

(Below) *Purple PASSION* was a late production P-47D assigned to the 513th FS, 406th FG. The vertical stripes on the aft fuselage were added just after the end of the war. The 406th Fighter Group remained in Germany after the war assigned to the Allied Army of Occupation. (R. C. Jones via Larry Davis)

(Above) Groundcrew prepare Capt Jay C. van Bloom's *BLOOM'S TOMB* for refueling. Capt van Bloom was assigned to the 514th FS, 406th FG. The swastikas under the cockpit sill are red, while the fuselage code has a thin yellow outline. A 150 gallon drop tank rests in the foreground. (John J. Quincy via Stanley Wyglendowski)

(Below) Capt van Bloom flew nine different *BLOOM'S TOMB*s. Three of the nine were lost in crashes by other pilots. This is number six. It lost almost five feet of the starboard wing on 22 October 1944 when another pilot hit a steel post while strafing a rail marshaling yard. (Lt Col S. J. Wyglendowski)

The 12th Air Force

The 12th Air Force was activated at Bolling Field, Washington DC on 20 August 1942. During August and September of 1942, the 12th AF moved to England under the command of Maj Gen James H. Doolittle who had recently returned from his attack on Japan using carrier borne B-25 Mitchell bombers. Tasked with supporting OPERATION TORCH, the Allied invasion of Algeria and French Morocco, the 12th and its subordinate units moved to North Africa during November of 1942. The 12th served with the Northwest African Air Forces from February through December of 1943 and then with the Mediterranean Allied Air Forces (MAAF) until the war's end.

The 12th AF fielded six P-47 groups during the war. These aircraft accounted for 141 victories, but their main contribution was in the tactical role where they destroyed enormous amounts of vital supplies and equipment, cut communications lines, knocked out troop and armor concentrations, and destroyed railroad lines and rolling stock wherever they were found. In essence, the 12 AF P-47 groups were the MTO's counterpart to the 9th AF P-47 groups operating in northwest Europe.

27th Fighter Group

The 27th FG originally began as the 27th Bombardment Group (Light) on 22 December 1939, but was not manned until 1 February 1940 at Barksdale Field in Louisiana. The Group sailed for the Philippines on 1 November 1941 and was to have been equipped with A-24s, however, due to the attack on Pearl Harbor the aircraft were diverted to Australia. The Group CO and twenty pilots were flown from Luzon to Australia to pick up these aircraft, but due to the deteriorating situation in the Philippines some of the pilots were diverted to Java while the remainder joined other new units. The 27th BG(L) was essentially reduced to a 'paper' unit when it was transferred back to the Zone of the Interior during May of 1942.

The remanned 27th BG(L) was re-equipped with the Douglas A-20

This P47D-28-RA of the 522nd FS, 27th FG displays the units rather simple markings — a red spinner, alternating red cowl flaps, and a single large aircraft letter on the fuselage side. (Author)

twin-engine attack bomber and trained in the US until it was ordered to North Africa during November of 1942. In Africa, the Group converted to the North American A-36 dive bomber and began combat operations with the 12th Air Force during June of 1943 and was designated the 27th Fighter-Bomber Group the following August. During May of 1944 the Group was redesignated the 27th Fighter Group and one month later the three squadrons (522nd, 523rd, and 524th) converted to the Republic P-47. Col Stephen B. Mack was the Group Commander during the P-47 era, but was replaced by Lt Col William R. Nevitt who led the Group until the end of the war.

The Group took part in the invasion of southern France (OPERATION DRAGOON) and supported the US 7th Army's drive up the Rhone River valley. On 4 September 1944 the Group flew 13 missions and 58 operational sorties despite having to operate from Santa Maria, Italy — over 200 miles from the combat zone. The distance required the use of drop tanks. Due to a shortage of the tanks, the Group had to bring them back as well. Flying low through intense ground fire to attack rail and road traffic, the 27th lost two Thunderbolts and had 10 badly damaged. The Group destroyed 107 motor vehicles, 30 horse drawn field artillery guns, 12 locomotives and stalling 11 trains some carrying heavy artillery guns. The attacks severely hampered the Germans' ability to conduct an orderly, cohesive withdrawal. The 27th FG's efforts resulted in their being awarded their fifth DUC of the war.

The 27th FG next concentrated on disrupting German communications in northern Italy and later took part in the Allied drive through southern France into Germany during the waning months of the war. The Group operated as a member of the 1st Tactical Air Force from 21 February 1945 until the end of the war.

Operating in the tactical role, the Group did not have an opportunity to compile a long list of enemy aircraft destroyed. The Group total stood at ten, with five each claimed by the 522nd and 523rd Fighters Squadrons.

Most of the 27th FG Jugs were left in their delivery scheme of natural metal. The unit markings were kept rather simple. The 522nd FS carried a red band on the fin and rudder. Every other cowl flap was also painted red. A large aircraft letter was carried on the fuselage. The 523rd FS carried a blue band on the fin and rudder, but placed the aircraft letter on the fin. The 524th FS used a yellow band on the tail surfaces and also placed the aircraft letter on the vertical fin.

57th Fighter Group

Formation of the 57th Pursuit Group was authorized on 20 November 1940 and its personnel were assigned to it at Mitchell Field, NY on 15 January 1941. Training was begun on Curtiss P-40s. The Group was redesignated the 57th Fighter Group during May of 1942 and was sent to the Middle East to train with the RAF. The 57th FG became operational during October and began operating in the Western Desert where it joined the 12th Air Force during August of 1943.

The Group was made up of the 64th Fighter Squadron (The Black Scorpions), the 65th FS (Fighting Cocks), and the 66th FS (Exterminators). The 66th FS took their name from an Axis Sally broadcast after the 'Palm Sunday Massacre' on 18 April 1943. Dozens of Luftwaffe Ju 52 transports loaded with troops and supplies were intercepted while over the Mediterranean Sea on their way to North Africa. Most were shot down. During her broadcast, Axis Sally promised that the Luftwaffe would deal with the cowardly *"Squadron X"* for shooting down unarmed transports. The Group converted to P-47s during December of 1943 while under the command of Col Archibald J. Knight.

The 57th FG was the first 12th AF unit to both convert to the P-47 and pioneer its use as a low level strafer and dive bomber. OPERATION STRANGLE, an air operation designed to interdict German supplies moving to the front lines in Italy, was put into operation to aid the ground forces' drive on Rome on 19 March 1944. The 57th FG moved from Italy to a new base on the island of Corsica on 30 March where it was to operate as a task force and put up at least 48 fighter-bomber sorties per day while acting as its own top cover. During the period from 1 April through 14 April 1944 the Group averaged 80 sorties per day and on 14 April reached a peak of 91 sorties between 0800 and 1610 hours while flying six missions into the Florence-Arezzo area. Dive bombing attacks sealed two tunnels, destroyed a rail bridge, six locomotives, 108 rail cars, cut the railroad tracks at nine spots, and burned an oil dump. The Group also managed to tangle with a gaggle of Me 109s and Fw 190s. The formation of 12 Jugs claimed three German fighters and one probable for the loss of one P-47. The day's activity earned the Group a DUC.

The 57th FG played a vital tactical role in the French campaign against the island of Elba during June of 1944 and the invasion of southern France the following August. The Group then concentrated on providing support and interdiction missions against the Germans and their remaining Italian allies in northern Italy from September until May of 1945. The nature of the group's tactical operations also meant several moves along the Italian Peninsula during 1944 and 1945. The Group found temporary homes in Amendola, Corcola, the island of Corsica, Omborne Air Field, Grosseto (twice), Villafranca di Verone, and Bagnoli.

The Group amassed 30 victories while flying the P-47. The 66th FS led the Group with 16, followed by the 65th with eight, and the 64th FS with six. 1Lt John J. Leniham of the 64th FS was the high scorer with three kills, followed by his squadron mate 1Lt Paul L. Carll with two. 1Lt Harold T. Monahan and his two victories topped the 65th FS, and 2Lt H. W. Cleveland and 1Lt G. Kriss each had a pair of victories with

ANNE was a P-47D-25-RE assigned to the 64th FS, 57th FG. *ANNE's* Pratt & Whitney R-2800 radial engine turned a Hamilton-Standard propeller. (Author)

Ponnie was a member of the 'Black Scorpions' — the 64th FS of the 57th FG. The P-47D-28-RA carries the squadron emblem on her cowl and a yellow outline black aircraft number on her fuselage side. A battery cart has been plugged into the electrical receptacle on the far side of the fuselage. (Fred Bamberger via P. M. Bowers)

(Above) *Billie* was assigned to the 57th FG's 65th FS — 'The Fighting Red Cocks'. *Billie* is carrying a bundle of three 4.5-inch rocket tubes under her port wing. (Author)

the 66th Fighter Squadron.

The 57th FG's first batch of P-47s was delivered and flown in olive drab over neutral gray camouflage. The later bubble-canopied P-47s were left unpainted. Most of the aircraft, both Razorbacks and Bubble-tops, carried a red cowl ring as a theater recognition marking. The aircraft also carried yellow bands with a thin black outline on the wings, vertical fin, and rudder. The Squadron's aircraft numbers were placed on the fuselage just ahead of the national insignia — the **64th FS** used **10 through 39**, the **65th 40 through 69**, and the **66th FS 70 through 99**. The **HQ Flight** was assigned **1 through 9**. The numbers were white on olive drab finished aircraft and black on the natural metal aircraft. Additionally, some of the aircraft used a thin outline or shadow on the fuselage numbers.

All of the squadrons carried their insignia on the cowls. The 64th FS insignia consisted of a black scorpion against a pyramid background, the 65th FS featured a red rooster wearing a shamrock around its neck, and the 66th FS carried a fighting cock on an oval background. Additionally, the 66th's insignia was superimposed on a large X — a carryover from the squadron's earlier use of the P-40 (and the origin of the name 'Squadron X' in Axis Sally's broadcast).

Jeanie, a P-47D-30-RE assigned to the 65th FS, 57th FG bores over the bombed out buildings of Hitler's Eagle's Nest. The Eagle's Nest was built on a mountain at Bertchesgaden in southeastern Bavaria, just across the border from Salzburg, Austria. (Author)

"Tiny Jem" was a razorbacked P-47D assigned to the 57th FG's Exterminators. The 66th FS adopted the name and made it part of their insignia when Axis Sally called them 'Squadron X' during a radio broadcast. (Fred Bamberger via P. M. Bowers)

Billie was apparently a popular name in the 57th FG. This *Billie* is a P-47D-28-RA assigned to the 66th FS — the 'Exterminators'. The Squadron badge, a boxing rooster, was superimposed on a large 'X' painted on the cowl.

"AY CHIUHUAHUA" landed at the 325th FG's base due to low fuel. The P-47D-28-RE was assigned to the 66th FS, 57th FG. (Stan Wilson)

79th Fighter Group

The 79th Pursuit Group was established on 13 January 1942 and activated at Dale Mabry Field, near Tallahassee, Florida on 9 February 1942. Its subordinate squadrons were the 85th, 86th, and 87th Pursuit Squadrons. The Squadrons later took the names 'Flying Skulls', 'The Comanches', and 'Skeeters' respectively. The Group was redesignated the 79th Fighter Group during May of 1942.

After training with P-40s the 79th FG was ordered to join the 9th Air Force in the Mid-East under the command of Lt Col Peter McGoldrick, a West Point graduate, with Maj Earl E. Bates as his Operations Officer. Later, Lt Col McGoldrick would be the first member of the Group to die in combat. The 79th FG took part in the North African Campaign and, when the 9th AF was sent back to England, the 79th FG was transferred to the 12th AF. After the McGoldrick's death in November of 1943, Maj Bates assumed command of the Group. On the 13 February 1944 (now) Col Bates became one of the first to be checked out in the P-47.

The 86th FS had the honor of flying the Group's first Thunderbolt mission on 9 March 1944 when Capt Risden Wall led eight P-47s on a patrol over Anzio. On 15 March the Group joined the assault on Monte Cassino and celebrated St Patrick's Day by scoring its first victory using the Jug when Capt Carl Stewart flying *"West By Gawd, Virginia"* shot down an Me 109 near Roecasecca, Italy. Capt Stewart, leading the 85th FS again on the 30 April, had several Free French pilots flying with the Squadron. Stewart and Lt Pierre Guoachon of the Lafayette Escadrille each flamed an Fw 190. On 15 April the 79th FG recorded a first when three P-47s of the 86th FS, each carrying a pair of 1000 lb bombs and a 500 pounder, hit a target in the Cassino area.

Beginning in April the Group underwent a number of command changes. Col Bates was replaced on 21 April 1944 by Col Charles W. Stark. Stark was shot down and taken prisoner 16 days later on 7 May. Lt Col Melvin J. Nielson took over on 12 May and served until he was relieved by Col Gladwyn E. Pinkston on 28 November 1944 (Pinkton remained in the position until the end of the war). It was also during April of 1944 that the weather was marginal for most of the month. Despite this, the 79th FG managed to fly 168 missions with 89 of them in the low level fighter bomber role.

OPERATION DRAGOON, the Allied invasion of southern France, was launched on 15 August 1944. By 0715 hours the 79th FG had already flown 14 mission before the assault troops had hit the beaches. They added another four before noon while flying from Serragia, Corsica.

The 79th FG was then shifted back to the 'Desert Air Force' and moved to Jesi on 3 October to work with the British 8th Army. The 79th added air-to-ground rockets to their arsenal, becoming the first group on the 8th Army's front to carry six rockets (three to a side) in tubes under their wings. They flew their first rocket mission on 19 October. On the 13 October the Group flew the first of many missions over Yugoslavia in support of the Russian drive through the Balkans. During December of 1944 severe weather greatly limited most operations.

The Group flew its 30,000th combat sortie during January of 1945. The mission was flown by Lt Col Johnny Martin who flew *10 Grand*, Republic's 10,000th P-47. Martin flew over 200 combat missions. After the war he went missing over the Atlantic Ocean while flying a P-51 with the Virginia Air National Guard.

(Above) XO1, assigned to the HQ Flight of the 79th FG, banks away from a pair of P-47s of the 85th FS 'Flying Skulls' P-47s. The three yellow lightning bolts and pale blue vertical fin and rudder were added during the spring of 1945. (Col R. M. Hoffman)

KOOLEY'S KOMET was flown by Lt Ed Kelly of the 87th FS 'Skeeters'. Kelly and his *KOMET* were part of the 79th Fighter Group. A 500 lb bomb is shackled under the starboard wing. (Woerpel via Graser)

10 Grand was the 10,000th P-47 Thunderbolt delivered to the USAAF. It was flown to a special delivery ceremony by Women's Air Service Pilot (WASP) Theresa James. *10 Grand* was later assigned to the 87th FS, 79th FG and flew its first sortie on 19 January 1945 piloted by Col John Martin, CO of the 79th. (Norris Graser)

MISS BETTE II of the 87th FS, 79th FG sits on the brick ramp at München/Riem Airport, Germany in 1945. The 'X98' on the fuselage has been stenciled on. (J. V. Crow)

A bare metal P-47D of the 525th FS, 86th FG prepares for a mission while another pilot and an Army nurse pose for the camera. The red and white striped vertical fin meant many of the Group's Thunderbolts had their serial numbers moved to the fuselage. (R. Hoffman)

(Below) Maj John H. Buckner flew the *De Old Man* as commander of the 527th FS, 86th FG. During the late 1970s and early 1980s, the 527th was resurrected as the 527th Aggressor Squadron, flying Northrop F-5E Tiger IIs out of RAF Alconbury, UK. (Author's Collection)

The 79th FG's tactical missions continued through the winter and spring of 1945. For seventeen straight days the Group put up over 100 P-47s each day and, from 16 through 20 April, their daily sortie rate reached over 160. The Group received a DUC for their actions during this period. From April 25th through 1 May they roamed at will over northern Italy shooting up any targets they could find. The mission flown on 1 May proved to be their last.

The 79th Fighter Group finished the war with 29 victories, 4 probables, and 20 damaged while flying the Thunderbolt. The 86th and 87th both had 12 victories, the 85th had four, and the HQ Flight one. Three pilots each had a pair of kills — Capt Carl Stewart of the 85th, and Lts Charles Hancock and Billy Head of the 86th.

The Group flew both the standard camouflaged and natural metal finish Jugs. Each P-47 was assigned numbers — **XO1-X09 for the HQ Flight, X10 to X39 for the 85th, X40 through X69 for the 86th, and X70 to X99 for the 87th.** These numbers were 30 inches high and appeared on the fuselage sides in black stencil or solid style. A few aircraft had a yellow outline around the numbers. During the spring of 1945 the Group painted the fin and rudders pale blue and three yellow lightning bolts in fan-shaped arrangement. Some aircraft also had their horizontal stabilizers painted pale blue. Call signs were 'Dickey' for the 85th, 'Crowfoot' the 86th, and 'Tadpole' for the 87th.

86th Fighter Group

The 86th FG came into being as a Bombardment Group (Light) on 13 January 1942 with activation the following month on 10 February at Will Rogers Field, Oklahoma. The Group was redesignated the 86th Bombardment Group (Dive) on 13 January 1943 followed by another name change to the 86th Fighter-Bomber Group during August of 1943. The Group finally settled down as the 86th Fighter Group in May of 1944. The Group was assigned the 525th, 526th, and 527th Squadrons. The 86th moved to North Africa during the Spring of 1943 to join the 12th AF and became combat operational flying A-36 Apaches the following July — participating in the invasions of Sicily and southern Italy. The A-36s were replaced with P-47s during 1944 as the Allies were attempting to drive toward Rome. Their assigned targets included convoys, trains, shipping, ammunition dumps, troop and supply depots, bridges, rail lines, and rolling stock. They also flew patrols and interdiction missions.

The Group's next assignment was to cover the Allied landings in southern France during August of 1944. From September of 1944 through April of 1945, the bulk of the missions were concentrated on eliminating the Axis' lines of communication throughout northern Italy. The 86th also became a part of the 1st Tactical Air Force on 21 February 1945. Finished in Italy, the 86th FG went to work on the railroads of Germany during April and May of 1945.

Over the course of 1944 and 1945, the 86th FG earned two DUCs. The first DUC resulted from their actions on 25 May 1944 when the Group flew through intense ground fire to hit German troops and vehicles trying to halt the Allies' drive on Rome. The second DUC was awarded for action against German airfields and convoys in northern Germany on 20 April 1945 disorganizing the German retreat in that area. The 86th remained in Germany as part of the occupying forces.

The Group had a total of 12 P-47 victories in the air. The 526th FS had seven and the 527th FS was credited with five. Lt Beringer A. Anderson of the 526th Fs and Lt Leonard P. Milton of the 527th FS each scored a pair of victories. In keeping with their close support role, the 86th FG was constantly on the move to forward bases in Sicily, Italy, Corsica, France, and finally Germany as the Allies pursued the retreating German Army across the face of Europe.

Markings for the 86th were fairly simple — the P-47s wore a red cowl ring and prop boss, while a few also had red cowl flaps. Squadron numbers were **10 to 39 for the 525th**, **40 through 69 for the 526th**, and **70 to 99 for the 527th**, and **1 through 9 for the HQ Flight**. The Group later applied seven red horizontal stripes over the entire white painted tail surfaces — a design which earned them the name 'Candy Stripers'. Since the stripes covered the serial numbers on the tail, the numbers were repeated on the fuselage sides in front of the US insignia.

324th Fighter Group

The 324th FG became a part of the USAAF on 24 June 1942 and was activated at Mitchell Field, New York on 6 July 1942 and equipped with P-40s. It was ordered to the Middle East the following October. The final elements arrived there during December of 1942 to begin operations with the 9th Air Force. The three squadrons, the 314th, 315th and 316th, were initially parceled out to other units to gain experience. The Squadrons were reunited with the Group in Tunisia during June of 1943.

The 324th FG was transferred to the 12th AF and renewed their operations on 30 October 1943. Flying in the tactical role, the Group hit roads, rail lines, bridges, marshaling yards, supply depots, motor vehicles, artillery positions, troop concentrations, and targets of opportunity. In Italy the 324th FG protected the landings at Anzio before converting from the P-40 to the P-47 during July of 1944 in time to support the assault on Southern France in August. The Group then helped in the reduction of the Colmar bridgehead and supported the US 7th Army's drive through the Siegfried Line in March of 1945. The 324th was awarded the French Croix de Guerre with Palm for supporting the French forces in Italy and France.

The Group ended the war with 29 air-to-air victories. The 314th FS (Hawks) had 13, the 315th (Crusaders) had four, and the 316th (Hells Belles) claimed 12. The 314th's 2Lt Philander D. Morgan, Jr. was top gun with three kills followed by the 316th's 1Lt John W. Haun with two.

Overall, the Group markings followed the standard allotment of aircraft numbers and squadron colors on the natural metal P-47s. The numbers were normally painted black with the **314th using 10-39** and yellow, the **315th 40-69** and red, and the **316th 70-99** and blue. There is at least one instance of an aircraft from the 315th FS having the number painted in the squadron color with a black shadow. The aircraft numbers were placed in front of the fuselage insignia. The cowl rings were red. A flattened diamond was painted on the cowl and a lightning flash was painted on the fuselage sides using the squadron colors. Both were sometimes outlined in black or given a black shadow. A black band was painted across the fin and rudder. An isosceles triangle painted in the squadron color was superimposed over the front of the band.

White 39 was an olive drab P-47D-27-RE assigned to the 525th FS, 86th FG. The serial number (26787) in white has been relocated to the fuselage side due to the complete red and white striped overpainting of the tail surfaces. The 86th continued to paint red and white stripes on the tails of some of their F-16 Fighting Falcons when they were renamed the 86th Tactical Fighter Wing and stationed at Ramstein Air Base, Germany. (Author's Collection)

OLE BALDY was a P-47D-27-RE flown by Capt Botten of the 525th FS, 86th FG. Despite the 12 crosses under the cockpit sill, Botten is not credited with any official victories. The natural metal Jugs continued the tradition of repainting the serial number on the fuselage side — this time in black. (Author's Collection)

(Below) *Amy Lou* suffered a collapsed landing gear leg when she ran off a slick runway after returning from a mission. The P-47D-27-RE was assigned to the 314th FS, 324th FG during the winter of 1944 and 1945. The cowl diamond, lightning bolt, fuselage number shadow, and tail chevron were yellow. (G. Letzter)

A pilot awaits — somewhat anxiously perhaps — while ground crews refuel and rearm his P-47D-30-RE. The Jug is assigned to the 324th FG, but it is not clear whether it is the 314th, 315th, or 316th FSs. The knobby tires on the P-47 were useful when operating from often slick or muddy airfields. (E. G. Nicolle)

A 314th FS, 324th FG P-47D-28-RE undergoes extensive maintenance. In addition to the yellow lightning bolt on the fuselage side, a yellow wedge was inserted into the front of the black ID band on the fin. Seventy-five gallon drop tanks rest in the foreground. Open air stockpiles of fuel, bombs, ammunition, and some spare parts were a common sight at forward operating bases (E. G. Nicolle)

A loaded bomb cart rests in the foreground while groundcrews of the 316th FS, 324th FG rearm a pair of P-47Ds during the winter of 1944-45. The 316th FS carried blue lightning bolts on their fuselage sides. A regular cycle of rearming and refueling followed by another sortie against the retreating Germans was the daily routine for Jugs operating in the close support role. (E. G. Nicolle)

350th Fighter Group

The 350th Fighter Group was activated by the 8th Air Force at Bushey Hall on 2 October 1942. The Group arrived piecemeal in North Africa during January and February of 1943. The Group was assigned to the 12 AF during the entire war flying Bell P-39s and P-400s and a few Lockheed P-38 Lightnings before converting to the Republic P-47 during August and September of 1944. The 350th FG flew patrols and interceptions while protecting convoys and providing support to the ground forces along the coast of Algeria. The Group finished off its operations in North Africa during the Tunisian Campaign. After the fall of Sicily in July of 1943, the 350th moved to Italy and flew from fields in Corsica and Tarquinia. The Group supported the invasion of southern France during August of 1944.

The 350th Group produced the only Medal of Honor winner who flew the P-47 in the European Theater. 1Lt Raymond L. Knight of the 346th FS was awarded a posthumous Medal of Honor for missions flown on 24th and 25th April 1945. On those missions he personally destroyed 20 enemy aircraft on the ground and personally led the raids on air fields through intense flak. He felt that they had missed some aircraft so he went back the next day and was hit by ground fire. While attempting to nurse *OH JOHNNIE* over the mountains to return to base he crashed into a mountain and was killed.

The 350th FG was credited with 19 aerial victories while flying the P-47. The 345th FS had two, the 346th FS scored 11, and the 347th FS claimed six. The leading scored was Cap. Frank W. Heckenkamp of the 347th FS with three kills. Three pilots of the 346th FS — 1Lt Robert C. Tomlinson, Maj Charles F. Gilbert, and 2Lt Richard P. Sulzbach — each had a pair of kills. The Group Commanders during the P-47 era were Lt Cols Ariel W. Nielsen and John C. Robertson.

The Group's P-47s appeared in both olive drab and neutral gray and in overall natural metal schemes. The 350th also adopted an unusual aircraft identification for its P-47s. The first digit was the last number of the squadron, the second was the letter indicating the flight in the squadron and the third letter was the aircraft's number in the flight. This code was painted in small black characters on the fuselage forward of the national insignia on the 345th FS and 347th FS aircraft. Fighters in the 346th FS had the code emblazoned across the cowl and front fuselage.

The 345th FS used a lightning flash in a black stripe on the fin and rudder as a squadron marking. The 346th FS aircraft had a black and white checkered rudder, while the 347th FS carried a large letter A on the vertical tail surfaces. All three squadrons sometimes carried their squadron insignia on the cowl or fuselage sides. The 346th FS — known as the "Screaming Red Ass Squadron" — carried a kicking mule framed in V-shaped lightning bolts on its cowls. The 346th FS used the Disney cartoon character 'Goofy' flying an open cockpit P-47.

OH JOHNNIE was the olive drab mount of Lt Raymond L. Knight — the only P-47 pilot to win the Medal of Honor in the European Theater. Lt Knight, assigned to the 346th FS, 350th FG, destroyed 20 German aircraft on the ground in the space of two days. Hit by ground fire on the second day, Ray Knight was killed when he crashed into a mountain attempting to return to his base. *OH JOHNNIE*, a P-47D-27-RE, was named for his wife. (J. Robertson via David W. Weatherill)

(Above) This P-47D-25-RE of the 347th FS, 350th FG has been retro-fitted with a fin fillet. The '7C4' on the fuselage side indicates the 347th FS, C Flight, 4th aircraft. The Squadron was known as the 'Screaming Red Ass Squadron' for its kicking burro and 'V' insignia. (Robert Clifford Jones via L. Davis)

(Below) The P-47 held between 19 and 28 gallons of oil — usually on the inside. A flak hit cut the main oil line of Lt Edwin L. King's P-47D as he was strafing German gun positions. Soaked in hot oil, Lt King flew his crippled Jug back to base and landed just as the engine seized. It is interesting that King was strafing the Germans, was hit, and then nursed his crippled Jug back to base while still carrying his centerline drop tank. After an engine change and a wash, Lt King went back to pounding the Wehrmacht. (USAAF)

The 15th Air Force

The 15th Air Force was organized on 30 October and activated in the Mediterranean Theater of Operations (MTO) on 1 November 1943. It began operations on 2 November as a strategic air force in Italy with seven Bombardment Wings and the 306th Fighter Wing. The 15th AF conducted strategic bombing missions in Italy, France, Poland, Czechoslovakia, Austria, Hungary, the Balkans, and as Germany. The original commander was Maj Gen James H. Doolittle followed by Maj Gen Nathan F. Twining, BGen James A. Mollison and BGen William L. Lee.

The 15th AF had two P-47 Groups although one, the 332nd Fighter Group, only had P-47s for a short time. The 332nd FG received 325th Fighter Group's Jugs when the 325th converted to the P-51. The 332nd FG flew the Thunderbolt for about two months with some of the aircraft retaining the 325th's black and yellow checker tail marking.

325th Fighter Group

The 325th Fighter Group was activated at Mitchell Field, NY on 3 August 1942 and was shipped to North Africa during the months of January and February of 1943. Initially equipped with P-40s, the pilots were ferried to Africa on board the USS Ranger. The P-40s took off from the carrier and flew on to Cazes Airdrome near Casa Blanca, French Morocco to join the 12th Air Force on 19 January 1943. They went into combat on 17 April 1943 escorting bombers and flying sea sweeps from Algeria and Tunisia. On 22 September they began the transition to the P-47 — a process lasting through October. The first P-47 mission — a milk run — was flown on 14 December 1943 when the Group provided withdrawal support for bombers that had bombed the Axis airfield at Kulamaki, Greece. This was followed by seven more such missions until they got into a scrap over the marshaling yards at Verona, Italy on 23 December. F/O R. L Catlin shot down two Me 109s while Maj Herschel H. 'Herky' Green claimed another. The most famous Thunderbolt mission in the theater occurred on 30 January 1944 when Col Robert Baseler, the Group Commander, led 60 P-47s on a sweep ahead of the bombers. The Group flew up the center of the Adriatic Sea at an altitude of 50 feet or less to avoid radar detection. The Group hit the enemy airfields in the Villaorba area and caught the Axis aircraft as they were taking off to intercept the bombers. During the ensuing dogfight Maj Herky Green flamed six enemy aircraft, while the other three pilots in his flight, Lt George Novotny, Lt Cecil Dean, and F/O Edsel Paulk, each claimed another. Lt Roy Hogg shot down two using only 40 rounds of ammunition. The enemy lost 38 aircraft while the 'Checkertail Clan' lost two and had another two damaged.

Other large missions were flown on 11 March 1944 when the 325th FG downed 10 enemy aircraft over the Padua marshaling yards in Italy, and on 6 April when they claimed another 10 aircraft over Zagreb airfield in Yugoslavia. The last P-47 mission was flown on 24 May 1944 over Wallersdorf airfield. Six enemy aircraft were destroyed in the air.

The final record with the P-47 was 97 missions (57 bomber escort, 25 fighter sweeps, 10 withdrawal, and 5 penetration escort), 3,626 sorties, 280 combat hours, and 153 victories. The Group suffered 38 losses, but only eight of these were attributed directly to enemy fighters. Another eleven losses were listed as unknown. If the figure of eight losses is used, the kill ratio is an impressive 19 to 1. If the unknowns are added, then the ratio drops to 8 to 1. Enemy losses included 131 fighter aircraft.

Sixty-six pilots scored at least one kill with the Jug. The top scorer was Maj Herky Green of the 317th with 10 kills. He was followed by Lt Eugene H. Emmons with nine, Maj Lewis "Bill" Chick with six, Lt George Novotny with five, Lt Edsel Paulk with five. All flew with the 317th FS. Capt Bill Rynne of the 319th FS had five. Several pilots scored part of their total score while flying the Jug. Broken down, the HQ Flight scored one kill, the 317th had 78, 318th claimed 26, and 319th ended up with 48 victories.

The Group flew the P-47D-4, D-6, D-10, D-15, and D-16. All but a few were painted olive drab and neutral gray. The tail surfaces were given 12-inch black and yellow checks, hence the name 'The Checkertail Clan'. The cowl rings were given 12-inch red bands. Individual numbers were assigned to each aircraft with each of the squadron's using a broad range of numbers. The **HQ Flight used 1 through 9**, the **317th FS used 10 to 39**, the **318th FS 40 to 69**, and the **319th FS used 70 - 99**. The numbers were usually painted in white on the fuselage sides.

Colonel Chet Sluder flew *Shimmy*, a P-47D-16-RE assigned to the 325th FG. Col Sluder was the Group Commander during the spring of 1944. The cowl blaze and checked tail added a lot of color to the otherwise basic olive drab and neutral gray camouflage scheme. (Col C. L. Sluder)

Capt Bunn Hearn of the 317th FS, 325th FG flew *The Star of Altoona*, a razorbacked P-47D. Maj Herschel 'Herky' Green (foreground) used this aircraft to score six kills on 6 January 1944. The Jug is carrying 150 gallon drop tanks of the style more commonly seen on the twin-engined Lockheed P-38 Lightning. (Author's Collection)

An apparently appreciative ground crewman watches as Lt Don Kearns touches up the artwork on *"Dallas Blonde"*, a razorbacked P-47D of the 319th FS, 325th FG. This particular piece of artwork was also found on a few other fighters and bombers.

"Dallas Blonde" was named after Lt Kearns first wife. The intricate pinup was dressed in a blue suit and brandished a pair of... sixguns. The P-47D-16-RE was painted in olive drab and neutral gray and had black and yellow diamond checkers on the tail and square checkers on the cowl flaps. The white '81' on the fuselage side was repeated under the red cowl ring. The Jug is carrying P-38 style 150 gallon drop tanks. (F. Patt)

Foreign Operators

France

After the North African Campaign ended in 1943, the USAAF agreed to retrain and re-equip the Free French Armee de l'Aire in North African. By March of 1944, the French began to receive P-47Ds. During May the 4eme Escadre de Chasse with two subordinate fighter groups was established on the island of Corsica. The two Groupes de Chasse, the II/5 'Lafayette' and the II/3 'Dauphine', were each given 16 P-47Ds. During July of 1944 a third group, I/4 'Navarre' was also formed on the island. All three units moved into southern France after the opening of OPERATION DRAGOON as part of the First Free French Air Corps Tactical Air Force. The Groupes de Chasse performed the classic P-47 role of providing close air support to the fast moving ground forces — perhaps with a special vengeance since the French were pounding German forces on French soil. Even as the German Army crumbled, the French established new P-47 units during 1944 and 1945. GCs I/5 'Champagne' and III/3 'Ardennes' were formed during late 1944 and 111/6 'Roussillon' was formed in early 1945. All were equipped with P-47Ds. Eventually, the French P-47 units moved into Germany with the other Allied fighter-bomber units.

French P-47s were initially flown in olive drab and neutral gray, but this scheme gradually gave way to natural metal finishes in keeping with other P-47s being delivered to front-line units. French P-47s wore the national insignia, a yellow-ringed red, white, and blue roundel, on the upper and lower surfaces of both wings and the fuselage sides. A blue, white, and red rectangular fin flash was carried on some aircraft while others wore the pre-war vertical blue, white, and red stripes on the rudder. Most aircraft carried a unit crest painted on the fuselage side and carried a two digit tactical number on the aft fuselage — white on olive drab camouflaged aircraft and black on natural metal finished fighters.

Italy

After Italy signed a separate peace with the Allies in 1943, Italian AF units began supporting Allied ground operations using a variety of ex-Regia Aeronautica and Allied aircraft. Italy also received enough brand new P-47D-25s to fully equip two units — 5 Stormo and 51 Stormo. Most of these P-47s operated in a natural metal scheme.

USSR

The Soviet Union received an allotment of 203 P-47s under Lend-Lease. Only 196 were actually received with seven being lost enroute. Four were delivered by ship via the northern Atlantic route to Murmansk, three by the Alaska-Siberia route, and the rest via the Persian Gulf.

Brazil

The Brazilian First Fighter Squadron arrived in Italy on 6 October 1944 and was based at Targuinia. The Squadron was attached to the 12th AF's 350th Fighter Group as a fourth squadron. Sixty-eight P-47s were used to equip the 1st FS, but only 31 were used in combat — the remainder were held in reserve.

The squadron flew its first combat sorties on 31 October 1944 when the four flight leaders and the operations officer flew as wingmen to pilots of the 350th FG on five milk runs. They received the radio call sign 'Jambocks'. Six more sorties were flown before 2Lt J. R. Cordeiro e Silva was shot down and became the Squadron's first combat loss. The

1st FS began operating on its own on 11 November 1944. On 16 November the Squadron lost a P-47 when it collided with a C-47 that was filming a flight to boost the morale of the home front. The pilot successfully bailed out, however two of the Squadron's pilots were in the C-47 that crashed. This brought their losses to three pilots in 11 days — an unfortunate situation owing to their problems in obtaining replacement pilots. The 350th Fighter Group moved to Pisa on 2 December 1944 and the 'Jambocks' went with them. Both units remained there until the end of the war.

On 14 December 1944, the 1st FS's Red and Green Flights hit the Paschiera rail yards and destroyed 33 boxcars and 7 trucks, while Yellow Flight cut the Cremora/Mantov rail lines in several spots. The Brazilian pilots always pressed home their attacks with a wild fervor and often returned with bits of their targets embedded in their aircraft. One pilot, so intent on strafing a truck in a factory yard, actually flew through a chimney cutting it in half. By the end of January of 1945 the Squadron had flown 66 missions in 30 days and had destroyed 155 motor vehicles, 36 box cars, and 11 locomotives. Despite their small numbers — a single squadron — their contributions were almost as much as a full strength fighter group. The Squadron's last sortie of the war occurred at 0700 on 2 may 1945 when two pilots flew a weather reconnaissance mission.

During their combat tour the Squadron flew 184 combat missions, but had only 22 pilots remaining when the war ended. Col Ariel W. Nielsen of the 350th Fighter Group recommended the 1st FS for a DUC — an honor only accorded one other foreign unit, an RAF Squadron.

Brazilian P-47s used the standard US scheme of olive drab and neutral gray with their national insignia in the same locations as the US insignia. Each flight used a letter and a number for identification purposes using the letters A, B, C, and D to denote the Flight and a number to indicate the individual aircraft. These were carried on the cowl in white. The rudder carried a yellow and green stripe. A unit insignia was carried on the fuselage just aft of the cowl. It consisted of an ostrich with a gun on a cloud, carrying a shield with the Southern Cross painted on it and their motto of 'Senta a Pua!' which, depending on the translation, meant either "Hit 'Em Hard" or "Give 'Em Hell". The bare metal Brazilian Jugs carried the same markings with the cowl letter and number in black.

The French Lafayette Escadrille flew this natural metal P-47D-30-RE during the latter months of the war. Forty-five mission markers are painted on the fuselage in front of the unit's Indian head emblem. French Jugs also appeared in olive drab over neutral gray and often carried large pre-war style blue, white, and red rudder stripes. (SHAA via Georges Grod)

(Above) The Germans regularly tested captured aircraft using salvaged parts from other aircraft to keep them running. This P-47 was given the code T9+FK and a white, or possibly yellow, tail. It was assigned to the Luftwaffe Test and Experimental Unit at Rechlin and Hanover-Winsdorf.

(Below) German engineers have stripped down this P-47 in preparation for inspection and later test flying. The Luftwaffe routinely painted oversized German insignia on captured aircraft to prevent their being fired upon by German flak batteries. (Earl Reinert)

(Below) This captured Jug retains its olive drab and neutral gray camouflage. The US insignia has been replaced by oversized German crosses. The standard German fighters of WW II — the Bf 109 and the Fw 190 — were noticeably smaller and lighter when compared to Republic's heavyweight fighter.

(Above) After Italy dissolved its relationship with the Axis (or tried to), Italian forces operating with the Allies began to receive new equipment. These 5 Stormo P-47D-25s are lined up for an inspection after the end of the war.

(Below) Most P-47s sent to the USSR arrived via ship in the Persian Gulf and were then assembled and flown into southern Russia. This P-47D-27-RE was delivered in olive drab and neutral gray with delivery markings consisting of a red star on a white disk. Soviet use of the P-47 has been little documented. (Earl Reinert)

(Below) SOVEREIGN SENATORS K. OF P. , at a Soviet testing facility, was one of three P-47s delivered via the Alaska-Siberia route. The long flight over arctic wasteland mandated the addition of a direction finding loop antenna on the fuselage spine.

(Above) Brazil received 68 P-47s and used about half of them in combat. The remainder were held in reserve as replacements and for training. The Brazilian AF Jugs were a mixed bag of D-25s through D-30s and were attached to the US 12 AF's 350th FG.

(Below) Brazilian Jugs were camouflaged in olive drab and neutral gray. The Brazilian insignia emulated the general form of the US insignia — probably for quick recognition at a distance. Yellow and green stripes were painted on the rudders. D5, a P-47D-28-RE, has a row of mission markers stretching back to the disk on the fuselage insignia. (Jose Ribeiro de Wendonca via Jeff Ethell)

(Below) Shortly after the end of the war Brazilian Thunderbolts began to appear in natural metal. The blue disk and white bars of the US insignia have also disappeared. This aircraft was the sixth aircraft in A Flight. A red spiral encircles the propeller spinner.